Participate

DESIGNING WITH USER-GENERATED CONTENT

HELEN

Princeton A

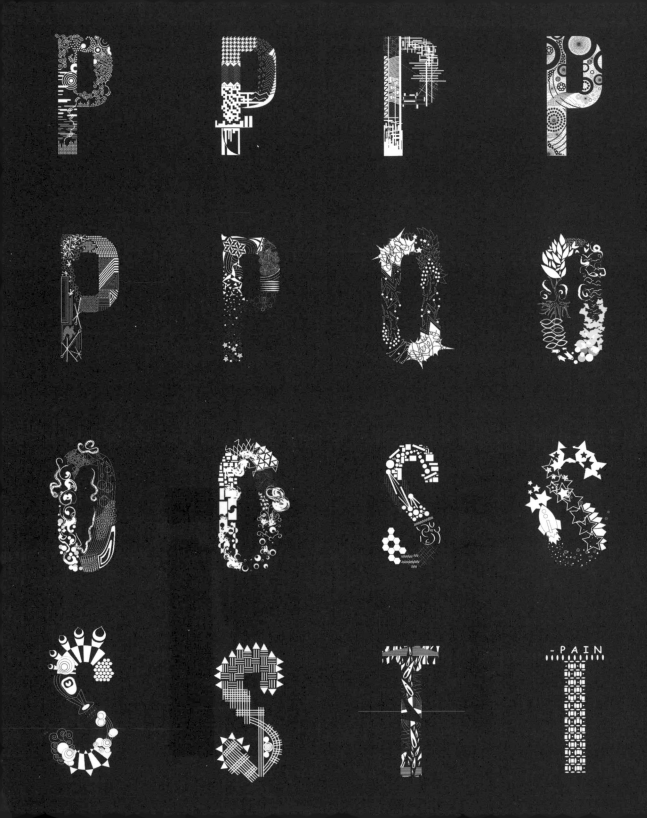

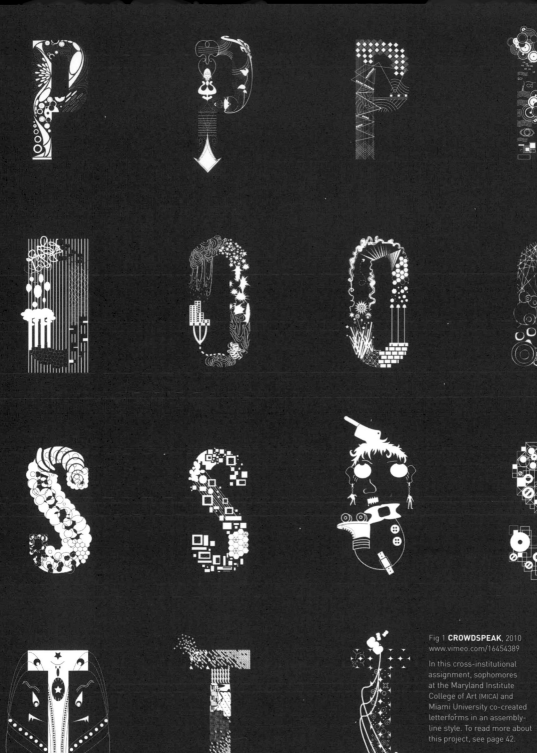

Fig 1 **CROWDSPEAK**, 2010
www.vimeo.com/16454389

In this cross-institutional
assignment, sophomores
at the Maryland Institute
College of Art (MICA) and
Miami University co-created
letterforms in an assembly-
line style. To read more about
this project, see page 42.

Published by

Princeton Architectural Press

37 East Seventh Street

New York, New York 10003

For a free catalog of books, call 1.800.722.6657.

Visit our website at www.papress.com.

Editor: Nicola Bednarek Brower

Designers: Helen Armstrong and Zvezdana Stojmirovic

Design Briefs series editor: Ellen Lupton

Special thanks to: Bree Anne Apperley, Sara Bader, Janet Behning,
Carina Cha, Tom Cho, Penny (Yuen Pik) Chu, Russell Fernandez, Jan
Haux, Felipe Hoyos, Linda Lee, John Myers, Katharine Myers, Margaret
Rogalski, Dan Simon, Andrew Stepanian, Jennifer Thompson, Paul
Wagner, Joseph Weston, and Deb Wood of Princeton Architectural Press
—Kevin C. Lippert, publisher

Typography: The earliest version of a DIN typeface was developed
by the D. Stempel AG foundry in 1923. DIN was redrawn by Dutch
typeface designer Albert-Jan Pool in 1995. Scala was designed by
Martin Majoor in 1990.

Library of Congress Cataloging-in-Publication Data

Armstrong, Helen, 1971–

Participate: designing with user-generated content /
Helen Armstrong and Zvezdana Stojmirovic.

    p. cm.

Includes bibliographical references and index.

ISBN 978-1-61689-025-4 (alk. paper)

1. Graphic arts—Technique. 2. Design—Social aspects. I. Stojmirovic,
Zvezdana, 1970– II. Title.

NC997.A689 2011

741.6–dc22

2011007788

CONTENTS

Fig 2 **HAPPY BLANK AND
BLANK YOU**, 2010
www.ellenculpepper.com

These letterpress notecards,
designed and produced by Ellen
Culpepper, provide a template
for user content. Rather than
dictating a message, they provide
an appealing visual framework.
Culpepper's cards demonstrate
that participatory design is not
limited to the digital world.

FOREWORD
Ellen Lupton

Q: Why did the graphic designer cross the road?

Graphic design, a discipline with a short history and uncertain future, has arrived at a busy intersection. More people than ever have begun to understand what designers do. Today, many everyday citizens know and recognize a variety of logos, brands, and typefaces. (Indeed, a company that seeks to alter a familiar brand image or package design risks sudden and merciless consumer revolt.) Whereas design once lurked at the edges of public consciousness, familiarity with its forms has become commonplace, breeding more congeniality than contempt.

The tools of design have hit the mainstream, along with its end results. Software is the gateway to the trippy world of making and sharing media. A little Photoshop can be a dangerous thing. Select, transform, filter, undo: for many designers working today, these intoxicating actions were our first taste of a medium that would quickly come to drive our lives. Meanwhile, the casual user or social tinkerer can now access the same basic tools and software as the hardcore professional. From digital scrapbookers to aspiring CEOs, today's design audience engages visual communication both actively and passively, uploading as well as downloading media, authoring content as well as consuming it. For those disinclined to host a blog or moderate a Flickr group, countless guides to "design thinking" entice the public to embrace the mindset—rather than the skill set—of design professionals.

A: To see where the crowd is moving.

Thus the harsh headlights of demystification have cast their beams across the fleeting forms of design practice. Digital tools and social media have exposed many creative industries to public interaction, causing a simultaneous valuing and devaluing of artistic expertise. The clients and endusers of designers, photographers, animators, illustrators, musicians, writers, and others have acquired a deeper understanding of once hidden creative methods; at the same time, they are looking for cheaper or faster ways to get what they want, often seeking more control over how they get it.

Contemporary designers create tools as well as finished works. A typeface, a website, a magazine template, a Wordpress theme: these instruments come alive in the hands of users: the client, the public, the giver, the taker; the butcher, the baker, the candlestick maker. Successful designers today produce not just packaged goods sealed with tamperproof lids but open-ended services that are one part psychotherapy and one part skill transfer—with some fortune-telling and massage therapy thrown in to keep the magic alive.

B. Because the future was chasing her.

The traffic is moving fast—in both directions. The culture of DIY and self-education that has incited frenzy among citizen journalists and amateur roboticists encompasses graphic designers as well. In a culture of diminishing resources and shrinking safety nets, DIY is the motto for us. Designers have learned to edit video, write code, and make coffee. We have become our own account managers, typesetters, and unpaid summer interns. Skills and thought processes that used to be the responsibilities of wholly separate jobs—such as animation and copywriting—have drifted into the designer's airspace, along with new areas of expertise, such as user experience and information architecture.

Whether you are a student or designer looking for fresh problems to solve or an educator seeking to energize your classroom with new processes and methodologies, this book will help you organize your mental toolbox. *Participate: Designing with User-Generated Content* lays out the new values that are shaping design innovation today. Concepts ranging from community engagement and modular construction to peer production and generative systems come to life through in-depth interviews with some of the world's leading practitioners. The book is illustrated throughout with richly described examples of work, from viral branding campaigns to experimental typefaces and interactive installations. Student exercises—illustrated with real results from real classrooms—will help any reader grasp the theory and practice of participatory design.

The authors of this book, Helen Armstrong and Zvezdana Stojmirovic, are gifted young educators who honed their voices as designers, authors, and teachers within the hands-on publishing culture fostered at the Maryland Institute College of Art (MICA) in Baltimore, an institution that has partnered with Princeton Architectural Press to produce an influential series of books about design processes. I am proud to have worked closely with Armstrong and Stojmirovic as students and colleagues; I am delighted now to see them embark on this ambitious independent endeavor. Their cross-country collaboration has yielded a timely and inspiring field guide to the new developments in design thinking.

C. Because she left her iPhone at Starbucks.

Today's graphic designer must prepare for a lifetime of education and reeducation. Much of this training will be picked up on the fly in real time. The experiences that users expected ten years ago have since evolved into new forms and protocols. Media and their modes of distribution are in flux. Mastery of a single technology or allegiance to particular hardware or software makes little sense in today's rapidly changing world. Designers must be both thinkers and makers, able to engage with a broad range of tools and methods.

What's your view of the current state of our field? Depending on where you stand, you might see a profession threatened by amateurs and automation, or you might see the blooming of a closed discourse into an open conversation. This book is an invitation to move in the direction of change. The traffic is dense. The flashing sign says run, don't walk. Find a break in the flow, and take a shot at it.

Fig 3 **WOOD WORK**, 2009
www.new.thingstosay.org/work/

Jürg Lehni created this installation together with Alex Rich to
produce text-based works citing
colloquial language. Users feed
words into the tool's interface,
initiating the production stages
of drilling and printing. Using
a CNC plotter, a rotated LCD
display, and an Apple TV, Wood
Work responds to user input by
drilling into sheets of wood to
form modular letterforms. The
initial production of text works
was followed by workshops
conducted with local schools
exploring how languages mutate.
A previous collaboration with
Rich called Empty Words, in
which letterforms were cut into
paper, led to the creation of
Wood Work.

WHAT IS PARTICIPATORY DESIGN?
Helen Armstrong

Graphic design is often about control—controlling what the audience sees, controlling the typography of a piece, controlling its concept. This interpretation of design stems from a modernist understanding of authorship. Closed and complete, a finished work delivers a specific message to a targeted audience. Participatory design turns this idea on its head.

Participatory design requires user content for completion. Rather than delivering clean, finished products to a passive audience, participatory designers are creating open-ended generative systems. Today's audience is changing. Viewers have become users, and professional creatives suddenly face a newly activated public. No longer content to simply digest messages, these users increasingly approach design with the expectation of having to fill in the blanks and actively insert content. The daily use of websites such as Vimeo, Flickr, Facebook, and YouTube has conditioned the public to contribute. And contribute they do.

The Birth of the Amateur Creative

Consumers participate because it's cheap, easy, and fun. On sites such as Threadless and Ponoko, they are encouraged to make their own products while relying on the production and distribution expertise offered by these sites. Using Lulu, the public writes, formats, prints, and disseminates publications. Both amateur and professional photographers inexpensively share their work through Flickr with millions of people. And blogs of all kinds threaten mainstream journalism as citizen journalists flood the web with free content.

This shift toward cheap online production and distribution does not seem to be ending any time soon. Chris Anderson, in his influential book *Free: The Future of a Radical Price,* points to Moore's Law, the long-term trend of increasing data density of computing hardware (and the related decrease of costs): "In a world where prices always seem to go up, the cost of anything built on [computer processing power, digital storage, and bandwidth] will always go down. And keep going down, until it is as close to zero as possible."[1] This decreasing cost of technology encourages the development of online, user-driven avenues for creation, which are further supported by emerging

1   Chris Anderson, *Free: The Future of a Radical Price* (New York: Hyperion, 2009), 78.

production methods that make small-run and one-off, customizable products and print-on-demand publications feasible.[2] Digital printers and rapid manufacturing diminish the economic advantages of large-scale production, thereby revolutionizing printing and production. The making of a viable product no longer requires a large up-front investment toward manufacturing and storing vast inventories. Gone are twentieth-century barriers to amateur creation.

As nondesigners busily create, designers too must get creative and make use of the new participatory spirit. This book reveals the myriad ways user participation both challenges and empowers professional artists and designers.

How Does Participatory Design Work?

The best participatory design solicits content from users—visual form, thematic content, physical movement or action—and then translates it into something greater than the initial contribution. In this way the designer provides value to users, rewarding them for their participation, typically in a nonmonetary way. The initial contributions are simple, easily carried out by the user: a photograph, a sketch, a doodle, a word, a movement, a vocalization, a touch. But when put into the context of a larger participatory project, user content flourishes in unexpected ways.

In designer Jonathan Puckey's project One Frame of Fame, for example, a small user snapshot joins with thousands of others—each responding to Puckey's parameters—to build an innovative music video. [Fig 35] Rarewords.org creator Mark Burrier illustrates words submitted by users for free, posting the results on his blog, in addition to selling them as prints. Designer Luna Maurer's Red Fungus project provides users with simple modules and instructions, inviting them to add to a large-scale user-generated exhibition. [Fig 81] Flexible identities, such as Wolff Olins's logo for New York City [Fig 55], Eddie Opara's Brooklyn Museum identity, and Andrew Blauvelt's Walker Art Center identity [Fig 48 and Fig 58], move even brands in a participatory direction, breaking apart traditional monolithic marks into systems that can be reconfigured by other designers or even, as in Post Typography's Splice Today identity, the users themselves. [Fig 49]

Participatory designers don't step aside; they enable. They aggregate, transform, and distribute user content, building user communities through their actions.

2 For a discussion of new fabrication techniques and customized manufacturing, see Chris Anderson, "In the Next Industrial Revolution, Atoms Are the New Bits" *Wired*, January 25, 2010, http://www.wired.com/magazine/2010/01/ff_newrevolution/ (accessed July 14, 2010).

Why Now?

The concept of participatory design was not born of the twenty-first century, although the new networked millennium has provided fertile ground. Early avant-garde art movements, such as Dadaism and Soviet Constructivism, experimented with social participation during the early twentieth century by urging viewers to join in mass spectacles.[3] In the 1960s postmodern values of open meaning, multiplicity, and disruption renewed interest in participatory art.

Theorist and author Umberto Eco, a pioneer of reader-response theory, wrote in 1962 that all works of art are open and, thereby, participatory to some degree: "Every reception of a work of art is both an interpretation and a performance of it, because in every reception the work takes on a fresh perspective for itself."[4] Each act of interpretation, in other words, completes its meaning anew. In his essay "The Poetics of the Open Work," Eco goes on to explore pieces that he considers incomplete in a more tangible way. These "Open Works," according to Eco, are "unfinished," and "The author seems to hand them on to the performer [user] more or less like the components of a construction kit."[5] In compositions by Karlheinz Stockhausen and Luciano Berio, Eco points out, the auditor collaborates with the composer in creating the work. It is this move beyond interpretation toward consciously involving the user in the making itself that points to the participatory projects of today.

Indeed, participatory movements popped up all over in the 1960s: Situationism in France, happenings in the United States, Neoconcretism in Brazil.[6] Contemporary participatory artists and designers can clearly be compared to Fluxus artists of the 1960s who provided instructions to others for making art.[7] The open works of these movements, however, filled an experimental, controversial cultural arena. Today participation has moved mainstream. No longer at the edge of art and design, it permeates not just the arts, but the general culture.[8] Advancements in technology have moved us from the postmodern to the participatory age.

Technology not only enables participation by providing easy avenues for contributions, it also shifts our mindset away from the individual toward networked, co-creative models of making. Two contemporary cultural movements opened the way for this inclusive approach: the open source movement and the copyleft movement.

3 For a discussion of Dadaism and Soviet mass spectacle, see Claire Bishop, ed., *Participation*, Documents of Contemporary Art (Cambridge, Mass.: MIT Press; London: Whitechapel, 2006).

   To further explore the politics of participation in the early 1900s, see Walter Benjamin, "The Author as Producer," in *Walter Benjamin: Selected Writings*, vol. 2, part 2, 1931-34, ed. Michael W. Jennings, Howard Eiland, and Gary Smith (Cambridge, Mass.: Belknap Press of Harvard University Press, 2003), 777.

4 Umberto Eco, "The Poetics of the Open Work," in Bishop, *Participation*, 22.

5 Ibid.

6 For a discussion of the 1960s and these three movements, as well as participatory art in general over the last one hundred years, see Bishop, *Participation*.

7 See discussion of Fluxus by Aaron Koblin, interview by the authors, page 65 of this book.

8 For more about participatory art's move into mainstream material reality, see Nicolas Bourriaud, *Relational Aesthetics*, trans. Simon Pleasance and Fronza Woods with the participation of Mathieu Copeland (Dijon: Les Presses du Réel, 2002).

The open source movement advocates free access to the source code of computer programs. In the twentieth century, traditional copyrights restricted such knowledge, preventing programmers from sharing resources. Activist Richard Stallman founded the free software movement in 1983 with the launch of the GNU Project.[9] In combination with Linux, the GNU Project became the first completely free software operating system, inspiring an ongoing spirit of mass collaboration among programmers, amateur and professional alike. The accessibility of its source code encouraged them to continually tinker with, improve, and hack the system. This process of aggregate making moved programming from isolated proprietary labs to vast networks of like-minded people, modeling participatory approaches for the general public. Thirty years later, graphic designers are following the programmers' lead, breaking the creative process into small simple modules that make it possible for vast numbers of users to contribute across time and space.

The copyleft movement sprang from the free software movement. Stallman led the way in developing new concepts of copyright that enable rather than limit the free distribution of information. Today Harvard law professor Lawrence Lessig continues this tradition.[10] A founding board member of the organization Creative Commons, he advocates flexible copyrights that allow content creators to reserve some rights but waive many restrictions on the reuse of information. Only through a revamping of intellectual property laws, Lessig maintains, can the free circulation of content thrive. And without the free circulation of content, participatory culture cannot exist.

Expanding more flexible intellectual property laws could further enable users to freely produce and share content, but such changes won't come about without conflict. As Henry Jenkins explains in his seminal book *Convergence Culture: Where Old and New Media Collide,* mass media privatized the production of content over the last one hundred years.[11] While technology bolsters the individual's ability to create, the corporate media, in particular, is reluctant to relinquish its monopoly control. As consumers transform into creators, our society struggles to accommodate them.

Of course, the tricky nature of aggregate authorship also requires a rethinking of intellectual property. Users must give up ownership of their contributions to participate in large collaborative projects, begging the

9   For more about the GNU Project and the free software movement, see http://www.gnu.org/. For more about the open source movement, see http://www.opensource.org/.

10   For an in-depth discussion of flexible copyright, see Lawrence Lessig, *The Future of Ideas: The Fate of the Commons in a Connected World* (New York: Random House, 2001).

11   Henry Jenkins, *Convergence Culture: Where Old and New Media Collide* (New York: New York University Press, 2006).

12 For an extended discussion of the negative impact of amateur creation, see Geert Lovink, *Zero Comments: Blogging and Critical Internet Culture* (New York: Routledge, 2007).

13 For an extended discussion of community, authorship, and participatory culture, see Vinicius Navarro, an interview with Henry Jenkins, "Sites of Convergence: An Interview for Brazilian Academics (Part Two)," *Confessions of an Aca-Fan: The Official Weblog of Henry Jenkins*, October 1, 2010, http://henryjenkins.org/2010/10/sites_of_convergence_an_interv_1.html (accessed November 28, 2010).

question of whether they could and should be compensated in some way. At the same time, designers question how they can share the source code of the open-ended systems they create without diminishing their profits.[12]

The struggle between corporate control and open source ideology, between protecting and sharing creative endeavors continues. As Jenkins notes, "Everyone sees that the future will be more participatory, but we are fighting over the terms of our participation."[13] This book does not presume to know the best terms of co-creation; instead it focuses on existing projects and considers the wealth of opportunities that activated users provide to artists and designers.

Upside-down, Bottom-up Design

Participatory design comprises a wide range of projects, but they all share certain aspects: community, modularity, flexibility, and technology are conditions inherent to participatory design. *Participate: Designing with User-Generated Content* focuses on one aspect in each chapter, providing a critical essay and a multitude of sample projects. These essays are followed by interviews with leading designers in the field, and practicums that reveal pragmatic applications of participatory ideas and expanded resources for developing your own projects.

This book reaches out to not only those excited by the possibilities of participatory design but also those frightened by it. Not only those intrigued by technology but also those intimidated by the range of technical tools and knowledge whizzing by them each day. We hope to give our readers ideas of how they too can experiment with the possibilities of user participation.

In the future, we believe, design will be scalable, unfixed, unfinished. In a world as vast, complex, and quickly changing as our own, designers can't respond fast enough by creating from inside silos. We must look to the user for contribution, celebrating the unpredictability of responses and enjoying the serendipity of process-oriented work. As designer and programmer Karsten Schmidt directs, "Stop thinking about design elements as objects and start enquiring what processes could lead to certain outcomes. It's the traditional approach turned upside down, bottom-up."[14] Through such bottom-up work, designers can thrive in participatory culture, reaching out to the vast pool of creative spirit that surrounds us.

14 Karsten Schmidt, interview by the authors, November 11, 2010.

Make a Statement

Photocopy and trim out copies of this template to create a modular signage system. If you want the large circles to fit standard office labels (one inch round), blow it up to 155 percent. The smaller circles can be filled in with color or patterns by hand. Construct letterforms using the big circles for large text and the little circles for small text. Distribute the panels to a group and then put them together to form a large display. Using this messaging system, encourage the group to express itself or promote a chosen cause. Let the modules become a catalyst for community.

Community

"OFTEN I SET UP A PLATFORM AND ASK A QUESTION, IN ONE WAY OR ANOTHER, AND THEN INVITE PEOPLE TO COME IN. IT'S A CONVERSATION, A CALL AND RESPONSE." KEETRA DEAN DIXON, INTERVIEW BY AUTHORS, 2010

Through participatory projects, designers establish platforms for social interaction. The give and take between user and designer (and between user and user) becomes an ongoing conversation. These conversations lead to connections, and connections lead to community in turn. Designers as community builders add value to and are valued by a public that is increasingly eager for engagement.

Strange as it may seem, the majority of users contribute to participatory projects just for the fun of it. In his seminal book *The Wealth of Networks: How Social Production Transforms Markets and Freedom,* theorist Yochai Benkler argues that the psychological satisfaction of making connections with other people is exactly why users bother to create and contribute content without monetary compensation.[1] In other words, the general public engages in these projects because people enjoy the community and creative fulfillment they provide. As Benkler explains, "For all of us, there comes a time...when we choose to act in some way that is oriented toward fulfilling our social and psychological needs, not our market-exchangeable needs. It is that part of our lives and our motivational structure that social production taps, and on which it thrives."[2] It is the happiness of belonging that drives users to contribute.[3]

Savvy creatives tap into this widespread generative spirit by developing projects that rely upon an infusion of outside content. Such works are open-ended, living on and on as users redefine them with each input. These projects run the gamut—from complex interactive installations to fill-in-the-blank silk-screened posters. We don't know exactly how many participatory projects exist, but we do know that they are growing exponentially in number. And the motivation behind them is primarily the longing for community.

1   Yochai Benkler, *The Wealth of Networks: How Social Production Transforms Markets and Freedom* (New Haven, Conn.: Yale University Press, 2006), 2–7.

2   Ibid., 98.

3   For a discussion of intrinsic motivation see Daniel H. Pink, *Drive: The Surprising Truth about What Motivates Us* (New York: Riverhead Books, 2009).

Consider, for example, Art House Co-op. Founded by Shane Zucker and Steven Peterman in 2006, this art initiative develops large-scale international art projects, such as the popular Sketchbook Project, which in its most recent iteration had over twenty-eight thousand participants. [Fig 5] For a small fee, Art House Co-op sends participants a Moleskine sketchbook, complete with a theme for filling their book. All of the resulting sketchbooks tour the country in an exhibition and then reside in the Art House Co-op permanent collection in Brooklyn, New York. These kinds of large collaborative projects become platforms for people to interact with one another, as they discuss contributions both online and in person.

Many of British designer Daniel Eatock's participatory projects stem from the online community that he first developed through his web portfolio template Indexhibit. After developing a portfolio site for himself in the early 2000s, Eatock, with the help of programmer Jeffery Vaska, began distributing its source code to create a network of people using the same format to display their work.[4] Eatock describes his original intent as the creation of "an archetypal format for a niche creative community."[5] At the time this book was published, around ten thousand people were using Indexhibit.

Eatock also invites his followers to contribute to various visual collections on his website. Through simple, quick contributions participants experience the instant gratification that comes from taking part in a larger collaborative effort. As Eatock explains, participants can see how "each contribution reconfirms the nature of the collection and suggests future directions the collection might take."[6]

Eatock's involvement in participatory culture goes back to the 1990s. His 1997 Utilitarian Poster, a silk-screened generic newsprint template, invites users to insert their own content. [Fig 6] Without viewer response, the piece is meaningless. Such physical artifacts emphasize that, although technology has pushed users toward a more active role, participatory projects do not have to be complex digital pieces. Studios such as Project Projects [Fig 11] and

4   For further discussion of Indexhibit, see *Daniel Eatock, Daniel Eatock Imprint* (New York: Princeton Architectural Press, 2008), 8–9.

5   Daniel Eatock, interview by the authors, October 7, 2010.

6   Ibid.

"TREATING OTHERS, INCLUDING STRANGERS, AS POTENTIAL PARTNERS IN COOPERATION CONTRIBUTES TO A THICKENING OF...SOCIAL BONDS BEYOND MERELY CO-CONSUMERS OF STANDARDIZED PRODUCTS." YOCHAI BENKLER, *THE WEALTH OF NETWORKS*, 2006

Fig 6 **THE COLOUR-IN DRESS**, 2008
www. berbersoepboer.nl
www.michielschuurman.com

Dutch textile designer Berber Soepboer created this customizable dress as one of four pieces for an exhibition about De Ploeg, a famous Dutch textile factory, in Bergeijk, a small Dutch village where the factory was originally located. Graphic designer Michiel Schuurman developed the black-and-white textile patterns, which are colored in by customers, using textile markers that ship with the dress.

Fig 7 **THE SKETCHBOOK PROJECT**, 2010
www.arthousecoop.com

The art initiative Art House Co-op instigates massive international collaborative art. For each project, founders Shane Zucker and Steven Peterman establish specific parameters and put out a general call for submissions through their website. Sketchbook Project, their most popular collaborative effort, had more than twenty-eight thousand participants in its most recent iteration.

(top to bottom) Sketchbooks from participants Ken McCarthy and Kate Castelli.

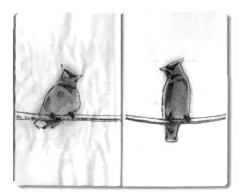

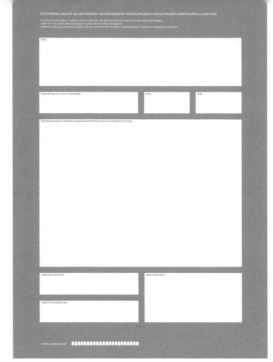

Fig 6 **UTILITARIAN POSTER**, 1998
www.eatock.com

A generic template silk-screened
on newsprint paper, Daniel
Eatock's Utilitarian Poster
methodically guides users through
the steps of creating their own
advertisements. It includes blanks
for inserting relevant information,
such as titles of events, images,
people to contact, etc. The work
completely depends on viewer
response for its essential content.

Fig 7 **THE DAILY MONSTER**, 2006
www.dailymonster.com

For his project the Daily Monster
Stefan Bucher turned a random
inkblot into a drawing of a
monster each day for a period
of one hundred days. He posted
these drawings on his website and
asked users to write and submit
stories based on the monster of
the day. Bucher made his drawings particularly compelling by
filming himself as he created each
one and posting the short videos
on the project site. Bucher later
invited people to submit their own
drawings based on his provided
inkblots.

MendeDesign [Fig 12] are, like Eatock, reenvisioning old production methods, such as silk-screening, letterpress, and offset lithography, as appropriate public forums for ongoing communal conversations.

In a society of individuals seeking connections and community, participatory designers and their clients can prosper as community builders. Participatory projects, both digital and print, take full advantage of existing social media networks, building social capital for both designer and contributors through user involvement. The resulting strong connections promote designer, client, or cause to a newly awakened crowd of amateur creatives.

Building a Consumer Base

Designers and their clients can profit from participatory projects not only through this creation of social capital, but also through more traditional revenue avenues. By inviting contribution, designers can build their own customer base.

San Francisco–based designer Stefan Bucher began his project the Daily Monster while waiting for a traditional publisher to accept a book proposal focused on his drawings of inkblot monsters. [Fig 7] While waiting for a response, he began the website dailymonster.com, where he posted short video clips of himself creating daily monster drawings and invited visitors to post stories for each monster. The response was overwhelming. After the initial success of the project, Bucher added a section called "Open Source Monsters" that allows people to submit their own drawings based on inkblots he provides. The online project led to a positive review by the book publisher and the publication of *100 Days of Monsters*.7 Before even hitting the stores, Bucher's book had a substantial group of potential purchasers consisting of project contributors.

7   Stefan Bucher, *100 Days of Monsters* (Cincinnati, Ohio: HOW Books, 2008).

Similarly, the London-based design studio Moving Brands built its own consumer base by creating one of the first examples of user-generated fashion. Through the website weare.movingbrands.com, the public could upload visual material, from which Moving Brands constructed a scarf pattern. [Fig 9] Users could buy the finished scarf online and in select independent design stores. The Weare Scarf generated a deluge of publicity both online and in the press. As in the Daily Monster project, participants coalesced into an involved consumer base before the product was even available for purchase. From the scarf project grew Granimator, a free iPhone application for designing wall-paper out of the Weare images (www.granimator.com/packs/9). Today nearly one thousand pictures have been uploaded by users. The Weare icons serve as a promotional tool for the agency and its products, and as an ongoing means for user creation.

Democratization of Media Culture

By providing outlets for user expression, participatory projects can perhaps even begin to democratize our media culture. As part of a promotional campaign for the 2006 MTV Europe Music Awards in Copenhagen, the London-based Troika, in collaboration with designer Moritz Waldemeyer, developed the Tool for Armchair Activists. [Fig 8] Set up as a fake protest against the music awards, passersby could text their thoughts to a powerful megaphone. A computerized voice then broadcast the messages to Copen-hagen's unsuspecting citizens. Over a two-week period, the machine received over 1,200 messages. The campaign promoted the awards, while allowing users to express their individual opinions.

The advertising firm ss + k also engaged text messaging in its participa-tory campaign for CREDO, a new mobile phone brand for Working Assets. [Fig 10] At select sites in San Francisco, pedestrians could text dialogue for public display in projected political cartoons. These projections forged links between progressive individuals, allowing local voices rather than corporate messages to build the brand and its community. According to the ss + k website, after three months of the campaign, 8 percent of consumers associated CREDO with "social responsibility" and 88 percent viewed the brand as a "worthy cause."

"WE FEEL IT'S A PRIVILEGE TO BE GIVEN A PLATFORM FOR COMMUNICATING, AND WE LIKE TO DISTRIBUTE THAT PRIVILEGE." ADAM MICHAELS, INTERVIEW BY AUTHORS, 2010

Fig 12 **TOOL FOR ARMCHAIR ACTIVISTS**, 2006
www.troika.uk.com

The experiential art studio Troika teamed up with designer Moritz Waldemeyer to create the Tool for Armchair Activists, a machine that broadcasts incoming text messages through its powerful megaphone, thus allowing arm-chair activists to protest from the comfort of their living rooms.

Together with MTV, Troika designed a two-week campaign around the Tool for Armchair Activists to raise awareness about the 2006 Europe Music Awards in Copenhagen.

Fig 13 **WEARE SCARF**, 2008
www.weare.movingbrands.com

With the Weare Scarf, the design studio Moving Brands created one of the first examples of user-generated fashion. Through a website, the public could create simple graphics to add to a gallery, which became the basis for Moving Brands's design of a scarf pattern.

According to Ben Wolstenholme, founder of Weare and Moving Brands, "Many people want to be involved in what they wear, and the creation of the world around them....The easiest way to think about this is 'Fashion 2.0,' it's an attitude not just a technology."[1]

1. Ben Wolstenholme, "Weare Press Release," Weare web-site, November 2007, http://weare.movingbrands.com (accessed November 29, 2010).

Fig 10 **SAY MUCH MORE, CREDO**, 2007
www.ssk.com

The advertising firm SS + K, together with installation artist Paul Notzold at TXTual Healing and production team Neverstop, created this text messaging campaign to promote CREDO, Working Assets's new mobile phone brand. At select sites around San Francisco, pedestrians could text dialogue for public display in projected political cartoons featuring George Bush and Dick Cheney.

Fig 11 **PRODUCTIVE POSTERS**, 2008
www.projectprojects.com

Project Projects's system of informational posters, developed for the Kounkuey Design Initiative's exhibition at the Van Alen Institute, grows through public participation, inviting users to write or draw their thoughts on the provided blank forms. Public participation is both the posters' subject matter and the essential means of fully realizing their design. Existing poster modules include case studies, quotations, background information, and supplementary research on participatory planning.

Companies interested in engaging grassroots organizations can thus use participatory culture to mold their brands out of individual voices and concerns.

Although the web facilitates the user's expectation of contribution, complex technology is not inherent to participatory projects. The New York–based design studio Project Projects, in collaboration with the not-for-profit Kounkuey Design Initiative, developed a participatory exhibition with the installation Productive Posters, conceived around a system of informational posters. [Fig 11] Each panel of the system was based on a template designed for inexpensive printing on standard office paper. The installation invited guests to write or draw their thoughts on participatory design on the provided blank forms, and add their panel to the exhibition.

Large-scale community projects such as those undertaken by Jessica Helfand and William Drenttel of Winterhouse Institute inspire users to gather content for social impact. During the 2006 midterm elections, Winterhouse Institute, in partnership with the AIGA, began the Polling Place Photo Project, a nationwide citizen journalism experiment in capturing democracy in action. [Fig 13] Winterhouse urged contributors to photograph their polling places on election day and add their images to a large archive as a commentary on voting in America. The archive currently includes six thousand photographs, representing all fifty states, as well as Americans voting abroad.

Participatory Design as Dialogue

Historically, the profession of graphic design has depended on traditional proprietary models of business that encourage the transmission of singular corporate messages—monologues. Participatory design replaces such monologues with conversations. Cultural critics suggest that these dialogues make messages less controllable and populations less easily manipulated by consolidated power structures.[8] As individual voices link together in communities, democratic expression strengthens and traditional models of business are threatened.

8   For a key discussion of the democratic potential of decentralized participation, see Henry Jenkins, *Convergence Culture: Where Old and New Media Collide* (New York: New York University Press, 2006), 240–60.

"SPEAKING TEACHES THE SPEAKER EVEN IF IT JUST MAKES NOISE." LAWRENCE LESSIG, *REMIX*, 2008

Theorist Jenkins sees the rise of participatory culture as "the reassertion of the practices and logics of folk culture in the face of a hundred years of mass culture." He explains, "We now have greater capacity to create again and we are forming communities around the practices of cultural production and circulation."[9] According to Jenkins, this new capacity to create, this rise of participatory culture, flies in the face of twentieth-century legal restrictions against the appropriation and recirculation of media by users. Corporate powers battle to maintain control, as mass media resists what Jenkins terms "media convergence."

Recent movements such as the free culture movement, the open source movement, and related flexible copyright licensing led by Creative Commons bolster the user side of such battles.[10] These movements speak to a new model of business that is less proprietary and more adept at utilizing peer production and co-creation than at guarding trade secrets. Designers can support these new approaches by establishing frameworks that amplify the voices of individuals.

For decades activists such as Kalle Lasn of Adbusters have pleaded with designers to answer for the societal damage resulting from frenzied advertising-driven consumerism.[11] The design community itself has called for more social responsibility through treatises such as the "First Things First Manifesto 2000"[12] or the more recent "Designers Accord."[13] By building projects that express and link individuals, designers can combat singular top-down visions of culture, making room for a multiplicity of voices eager for expression.

Participatory projects can serve as a profitable survival strategy for design firms in an increasingly DIY creative climate. If the designer-established parameters of such projects succeed, valuable communities emerge. On the best of days, these distributed communities can even act as a force of democracy within our society, wrenching cultural production from the hands of mass media.

9 Vinicius Navarro, an interview with Henry Jenkins, "Sites of Convergence: An Interview for Brazilian Academics (Part Two)," Confessions of an Aca-Fan: The Official Weblog of Henry Jenkins, October 1, 2010, http://henryjenkins.org/2010/10/sites_of_convergence_an_interv_1.html (accessed November 28, 2010).

10 For an extended discussion of copyright and culture, see Lawrence Lessing, Remix: Making Art and Commerce Thrive in the Hybrid Economy (New York: Penguin, 2008).

11 Kalle Lasn, Design Anarchy (Vancouver: Adbuster Media Foundation, 2006).

For a discussion of designers and social responsibility, see Steven Heller and Veronique Vienne, eds., Citizen Designer: Perspectives on Design Responsibility (New York: Allworth Press, 2003).

12 Rick Poynor, "First Things First Manifesto 2000," AIGA Journal of Graphic Design 17, no. 2 (1999): 6–7.

13 For more information on the Designers Accord, visit http://www.designersaccord.org/.

Fig 12 **I WANT YOU
(I REALLY DO)**, 2009
www.mendedesign.com

MendeDesign's I Want You poster
campaign, developed for SFMOMA,
had citizens compete to win free
political ad space. Winners were
provided with a wheat-pasted poster
campaign and two minutes of airtime
to broadcast their answers to the
central question of individual political
advocacy: "I Want You to…"

Fig 13 **POLLING PLACE PHOTO
PROJECT**, 2006–2008
www.winterhouse.com
www.pollingplacephotoproject.org

Initiated by Winterhouse Institute
in partnership with the AIGA,
the Polling Place Photo Project
began during the 2006 midterm
elections. Winterhouse urged
citizens to photograph their
polling places on election day and
then contribute to a large image
archive as a commentary on
voting in America. The New York
Times supported the project in
2008 and promoted it as a part of
their online election coverage.

STEVEN PETERMAN

www.arthousecoop.com

Steven Peterman and Shane Zucker, the founders of Art House Co-op, fly in the face of the art establishment by developing massive international art projects that welcome everyone. They began experimenting with participatory projects as students, underscoring their belief that anybody can be an artist. The art initiative has become known for the Sketchbook Project, for which participants submit filled sketchbooks to be exhibited nationally and then archived at the new Art House space in Brooklyn, New York. In this archive/storefront contributors can peruse what is fast becoming the world's largest collection of sketchbooks.

In Art House projects, everybody is welcome. You don't impose a curatorial role beyond the rules that you set up. Where did this idea of open participation come from?

We have always believed in it. We feel there is an elitist gallery world out there, and we don't want to be a part of that. This stems from me originally feeling like I couldn't even approach a gallery. I wasn't good enough. I realized then that there are many people of all ages, not just art students, who want to be involved in the art world and have no idea how to do it. We inspire them by just saying, "You can do this. Anyone can do this."

What role does community play in your work? What does it mean for you?

It's the whole thing. It's what keeps us going. It's what makes us unique. When we get all of these sketchbooks back, we'll have ten thousand-plus artist sketchbooks. I don't know any other gallery that has this many everyday people together in one collection. It defines who we are.

Do your projects set up a framework for people to interact with each other?

Yes. For example, people come to our sketchbook events bringing lists of people whose books they want to see. We ask them where they met them, and they say they met on our website. We don't even have a way to communicate on our site other than posting comments on people's images. Somehow people will find a way to communicate. They all talk and share each other's work, and then they come to see each other's sketchbooks in person. It's cool that we have created those little groups through our projects.

Participation is changing the larger art scene. Why do you think people submit work to your projects?

We get emails from participants who tell us they haven't done artwork in twenty years, and this has finally inspired them. That's awesome for us.

We also get people who want to be part of something bigger, in addition to doing artwork alone in a studio. They want their work to go towards something lasting. That's why we started the library. People make artwork for shows. It hangs on a wall for six weeks, and then it gets stuck in a closet. We want art to become a part of a community. A lot of people are attracted to that.

We also get people who use it as practice. They don't seem to have interest in anything else going on with us. Definitely the majority of the people, though, are the ones who want to be part of a bigger community and who want to be inspired by it.

Do you have any advice about how to structure a participatory project?

By far the Sketchbook Project has been the most

successful. I think it has something to do with the book format. It's a little more secretive and it's not just hanging on the wall. People like to let go and use it as something more than just making artwork. We get a better quality of work because they feel less restricted. We usually have just one rule, maybe a couple of things that make it easier for us when we have a mass amount.

Why are three thousand sketchbooks, or ten thousand sketchbooks, better than three? Is there ever going to be a point where the multitude will be too much?

We came up with the library to keep each submission together with these other ten thousand books or whatever it grows to. I am excited for the day that we have one hundred thousand books. For us it's not about the individual artist, it's about this group of artists that have come together. I don't think there will ever be a limit. We will keep getting bigger spaces to accommodate the endless amount of books that you can come see. People come in right now and sit there for hours looking through our collection. It isn't just three people and then you are done.

The submission fees provide a commercial underpinning to the site and to the projects. Do you see Art House as a sustainable source of income?

Yes, we are able to do this full-time. We have five employees, and it's a six-month-of-a-year business. Mainly, we make money when we are doing Sketchbook. There have been times when we were barely making enough to pay rent for ourselves, let alone the business, but we're going on our fifth year now. We just keep pushing and pushing.

We are not in it to make tons of money. We want to keep growing the community. The majority of the money goes back to the projects. The cost of traveling around the country with large exhibitions is enormous. I don't think people realize how much money we have to put into it to actually follow through with these things.

Your site encourages educational groups— organized school groups or just people who want to learn or do things together. What are the big lessons that you want students to walk away with?

We want to get across the idea that anybody can be an artist. I remember being in elementary school and feeling like the kid next to me was an awesome artist. I had an artistic drive, but I couldn't draw. It took me until I was a sophomore in art school to know that it's okay that I can't draw. It's important to know that you don't have to be a certain kind of artist.

It's interesting that Art House pairs a physical sense of community with the Internet platform.

This pairing is a direct reflection of Shane and me. Shane wants everything to be on the Internet and as high-tech as can be. I want to have a simple storefront where people have to come in and talk. I believe in the local community, people coming in, meeting us, and touching the books. That's one of the reasons why Shane and I work well together. We have shared goals, but different goals at the same time. We both push our own side. That's why we have such a diverse approach.

What are your plans for the future of Art House?

Right now we are setting up our brand-new storefront in Williamsburg, Brooklyn. It's going to add amazing accessibility to the library. We are becoming a destination that people want to come see when they come to New York, particularly people who have participated in our projects.

DANIEL EATOCK

www.eatock.com

London-based artist Daniel Eatock transforms design into an "open space for participation." User contributions often feed his projects, flexibly redirecting outcomes. In the early 2000s, he teamed up with programmer Jeffery Vaska to develop Indexhibit, an open source version of Eatock's own portfolio site. Approximately ten thousand people now use this platform. A graduate of London's Royal College of Art, Eatock works for clients such as Channel 4, a British television broadcaster, and the Serpentine Gallery in London. He also undertakes a multitude of self-directed projects.

Why are a hundred no-smoking sign photos more interesting than one?
One hundred dollars is better than one dollar. The more pixels, the better the resolution/clarity.

Is this desire to understand, through more pixels, what inspired you to start Indexhibit?
My original intent with Indexhibit has come true. It is ubiquitous and has become an archetypal format for a niche creative community. I would encourage everybody to try and improve things if they have an idea they believe in.

Your work transforms the process of community engagement into an artifact rather than a design byproduct. Was there a particular moment when your work shifted in this direction?
I remember making a drawing when I was sixteen on a beach in France. I was with a friend also called Daniel. He was fantastic at drawing. I tried to do the same, but my drawing never resembled the subject I was studying. On the beach one morning I gave up trying to draw what I saw. I took a clean sheet and

drew two horizontal lines across the paper, dividing it into thirds. In the top third I wrote "sky," in the middle third I wrote "sea," and in the bottom third I wrote "sand." The drawing was empty of content, blank, open for the viewer to engage and consider the content. I think it was the first time I made a work that was an open space for participation. This was probably the beginning of my interest in making things that people could either conceptually complete or literally add to and participate in the making.

What drives people to participate in your projects?
Most things are easy and take just a second—they have an instant gratification. Also I think people like being connected with a larger group.

A simple act can turn into a complex collaboration as communities form around making. This seems biological, cellular. Is there an organic quality to your work?
Yes, one thing informs the next. Each contribution reconfirms the nature of the collection and suggests future directions the collection might take. But I do not consider these works collaborative; I see them as participative.

What's the difference between collaborative and participative?
Collaborative suggests equal involvement—to participate is to take part in something bigger than any one part. My role is as an instigator of the work, and once the work builds momentum, I work as an editor, curator, etc.—I don't produce any of the component parts to these works; they are all contributed by the voluntary participants.

Abdul Hamid
Roman Milisic
Alan Murphy
Alexandra Roche
Alexis Taylor
Andrea Buran
Andy
Andy Rowbotham
Ashley O'Brien
Aurora Biancardi
Darren Barber
Darren Barber
Beat Raess
Tom Yard
Ben Harris
Ben Barker
Ben Hackshaw
Ben Hackshaw
Ben Jeffery
Boris Schandert
Carl Monte-D'Cruz
Carlos Maraver
Caroline Taylor
Charlotte Dumont
Christian Eager
Christian Eager
Christine Kline
Christopher Simmons
Clara Lilley
Craig Oldham
Damien Safie
Daniel Cuthbertson
Danielle Billings
Darren Barber
Darren Barber
Dave Lynch
David Dufour
Denis Kovac
Drew Heffron
Ed Price
Emily Usher
Eric Robinson
Filipe Cartaxo Silva
Giulia Miglioranza
Heidi Robertson
Jack Farrelly
Jake Pover
James Boynton
James O'Leary
James Ware
James Rush
Javita Retamal Benavente
Jean André
Jeffery Vaska
Jennifer Kennedy
João Parada
Joe Waller
Joel Priestland
John Bell
John Thomas Hudson
John Paul Dowling
John Roche
Jon Burgerman
Jon Lane-Smith
Jonty O'Connor
Joram Salisbury
Jose A Contreras
Joseph Hales
Julian James
Julien Bouvet
Justin Hutchison
Kevin Taylor
Lars Ivar Røed
Lee Henderson
Libby Lewis
Lina Hakim
Linus Kraemer
Lorenzo Cercellett
Louis Ferracane
Louis Mikolay
Luis C Pavón
Mario Ciaramitaro
Martin M Schilling
Mattew Gill-Brown
Maxime Delporte
Micah Panama
Michael McGuinness
Michael Rabinson
Mike Burrill
Monia
Natalie Shortt

Nick Jeeves
Nick Shea
Nicolas Abraham Apfelbaum Devincent
Nik Daughtry
Noah Hilsenrad
Oisín Share
Owen Jones
Paul Cleary
Peter Wright
Roman Milisic
Rowen Frazer
Sali Tabacchi
Sam Ely
Sam Mallett
Sanderson Bob
Sarah Boris
Sebastian Peetz
Senan Lee
Seong Lim
Steven Burke
Sonsoles Alvarez
Steven Harrison
Steve Rack
Stuart Weston
Sun Jung
Tom Crawshaw
Tim Water

Fig 14 **NO SMOKING SIGN LIBRARY**, 2007–ongoing
www.eatock.com

On his website Eatock invites submissions for this ongoing collection of no-smoking signs, providing alternatives to the archetypal sign. All signs can be downloaded and used for free in public and private places.

Eventually, Eatock plans to publish a commemorative poster to celebrate smoke-free England and mail copies to the first one hundred people who contributed to the library.

ADAM MICHAELS

www.projectprojects.com

Influenced by anarchist politics and the early 1990s DIY hardcore punk scene in Chicago, Adam Michaels works to extend his principles as a founding partner of Project Projects. In 2004 he established the New York studio with Prem Krishnamurthy. Rob Giampietro joined as a principal in 2010. Michaels sees himself as a translator, taking "complex thoughts and translat[ing] them into a legible form for wider audiences." Although heavily based in theory, his work is accessible, avoiding exclusionary approaches in favor of low-tech, resourceful methods of communication.

What is the role of community in your work?

First, while I'm speaking on behalf of the studio, I'd like to make clear that my views aren't necessarily representative of those of the other studio principals. While I see interaction with (and creation of) communities as an exciting aspect of the studio's work, this is less of a directed effort and more of a happy side effect. My approach to work comes from something of an anarchist perspective, in the sense of being part of a network of individual emancipatory practices, all conceived with an eye towards benefitting a broader community.

Can you describe some of your projects that invite audience participation?

Into the Open comes to mind first. In this architecture exhibition, held at a first-floor gallery space at Parsons in New York, we covered the walls with green chalkboard paint, stenciling display typography on them in black chalkboard spray paint. So every gallery wall was available for visitors to

mark up in chalk. This idea partially surfaced as a response to our perceived lack of public space for expression at Parsons—we thought that the exhibition space could also be a student forum. Speaking more generally, we're conscious that it's a privilege to be given a platform for public communication. Our design decisions are often made with the intent of distributing that privilege beyond ourselves.

How do you think print-on-demand and other tools for customization are changing our profession?

We've worked on a couple of print-on-demand projects, including a book series commissioned by Art in General. We produced a series of seventeen volumes documenting the artist projects produced through their New Commissions program. Each book contained a mixture of process documentation, research materials, final works, and commissioned essays. Simply put, the series couldn't have existed without print-on-demand technology; traditional printing for even a short run of the full series could have cost hundreds of thousands of dollars. And the books actually benefit from the resultant informality that can be difficult to achieve when financial stakes are high. While the material aspects of the books are difficult to love, the quirky production parameters pushed our design in some interesting, unexpected directions.

Are you passionate about finding low-tech ways to engage audiences, or do these solutions stem from the conditions of each project?

Both, I would say. I've appreciated inexpensive

production methods for years, starting with punk rock flyers, cassettes, records, etc. For these objects, it's impossible to untangle aesthetic effects from economic limitations, and the resultant sense of inclusivity—that anyone can directly participate in that culture—is genuinely liberating. More recently, at the studio, it's been important that our work hasn't overly emphasized technology. We think it's crucial to include all possible participants—not just those with the economic resources to have the latest consumer electronic device. Additionally, we tend to have affinities with various groups with limited economic resources, so the pragmatics of DIY production have carried through much of our work.

With the advance of the Internet and the democ-ratization of communication tools, consumers are now more activated and have more of a voice. Have you thought about that power shift?

I'm thrilled that masses of people now have the means to express themselves both instantaneously and internationally—though the sheer quantity of information can be exhausting to sift through. Thinking back to the 1990s, participants in subcul-tures often desired platforms for more widespread communication—at that time, something like a seven-inch record, pressed in a quantity of three hundred and individually mailed out, was then considered a useful means of transmitting mes-sages about a topic like veganism. In retrospect, this sounds fairly absurd as a means of communicating to a broad populace; however, myself and many others were profoundly affected by these objects, in a way completely unlike the way I receive informa-tion today. It seems fair to assume that this had something to do with the relative scarcity of records and zines, and the committed, complicated labors that were required for production, distribution, and

acquisition. Of course, this may be overly nostalgic on my part, and Myspace communiqués may well have similarly impacted youths of the early 2000s.

You are engaged in theory and you talk about anarchist politics. How do you negotiate such theory in your practice?

We've each read a good deal of theoretically informed writing over the years, and this continues to play an integral part in our thinking. When we entered our design educations in the 1990s, theory-based design discourse was peaking in America. The writing from this period was influential—I'm particularly thinking of Andrew Blauvelt's work— but I remember feeling frustration with the inward-looking nature of theoretical discourse. Instead, I wanted to form an outward-looking design practice, so as to enact theoretical concerns in the world at large. So for me, a crucial aspect of our work is the translation of theoretical or academic projects into unexpected forms that can be meaningful for wide audiences—this is the approach of Inventory Books, the series that I edit and design. I hope our work connects to a wide range of interested parties, regardless of whether they have a high-end educa-tion, a certain piece of technology, or any other accessory of privilege. We're aware of a long tradi-tion of designers—Otto Neurath, Quentin Fiore, and many others—that shared some of these concerns; we hope to connect to and extend this lineage. All of that said, on a day-to-day basis at the studio, we tend not to sit around discussing the finer points of, say, continental philosophy; the studio's pace is hectic, and the countless details of design work and sus-taining a studio tend to be—happily—all-consuming.

PROJECT PROJECTS

Fig 15 **INTO THE OPEN: POSITIONING PRACTICE**, 2009
www.projectprojects.com

(left) Project Projects created the exhibition design and graphics for Into the Open: Positioning Practice in collaboration with the design firm Saylor + Sirola. This exhibition, focusing on socially engaged architectural practices, was a restaging of the U.S. Pavilion for the Venice Architecture Biennale 2008, curated by Aaron Levy and William Menking. Project Projects developed a fresh design and presentation for this New York version. Transforming the exhibition's gallery space at Parsons The New School for Design into an open forum, they encouraged visitor participation by covering the space with green chalkboard paint.

Fig 16 **ART IN GENERAL**, 2009
www.projectprojects.com

(below) This print-on-demand book series documents artist projects produced for Art in General's New Commissions program. The inexpensive production, through the online self-publishing site called createspace.com, made the seventeen-volume series possible and created interesting design limitations.

Fig 17 **RE-SHUFFLE**, 2006
www.projectprojects.com

(above) Working with twelve graduate students from Bard College's Center for Curatorial Studies, Project Projects created this participatory catalog and exhibition. Re-Shuffle: Notions of an Itinerant Museum explores the responses of forty-seven artists and writers to the curators' prompt regarding the relevance of cultural institutions. In contrast to the traditional passive gallery experience, visitors assemble their own portable exhibition from the provided screen-printed boxes, stacks of cards, and mailing labels.

ERIC HUSBAND

www.collemcvoy.com

The strategic marketing agency Colle + McVoy creates traditional commercial campaigns—creative concepts, clever headlines, memorable imagery—but throws in an element of audience participation that takes them to a new level. Eric Husband, group creative director, explains that Colle + McVoy embraced digital technology earlier than most "and, in doing so, started to embrace what participation can do for an idea—and the results it produces."[1]

Did one particular project push your agency to use audience participation to build brands?
More than anything, technology has opened doors. YearbookYourself was a big breakthrough for us. It really integrated participation with social media.

Is the concept of community critical to your work?
Very. For Bikes Belong (www.bikesbelong.org), a Boulder-based advocacy group that promotes bicycling, uniting a community was our prime objective. In the case of People for Bikes (www.peopleforbikes. org), a passion for getting around on two wheels created a connection point. The shared passion of community cannot be underestimated when creating content around participation.

Is it hard to convince clients to involve the user in the final project?
Nothing is easy, especially when you're trying to crawl out of a recession. A media plan with guaranteed impressions might feel like a safer route than building a participatory experience. But as we use more dashboards and metrics to track results, it's getting easier. Even the creatives geek out on analytics here. For YearbookYourself, we knew

49 percent of users were clicking through to mall websites. Awards are great. But it's cool to know that your idea is working.

We recently built our own tool to monitor and analyze the volume of Twitter chatter. We call it Squawq. It gives our clients a snapshot of how a campaign is working on the social media front.

Share three key tips for doing a successful participatory project.
1. Technology is your friend. Embrace it. (But don't chase after every shiny new object.)
2. Make participation simple. Do they really need to be a "registered member" to participate? Eliminate barriers.
3. Don't force it. We've all seen our fair share of "Tell us your shoelace story" (or whatever product you're trying to sell) call to actions. People are participatory by nature, but we have our limits.

What do you hope/fear might happen to graphic design in the next twenty years?
Of course, there's this fear that design will be devalued as trends like crowdsourcing emerge. I sometimes fear that the design world is selling itself out, designing the next logo for a chance to win a five-hundred-dollar gift certificate. But I think these fears are unfounded. As long as the profession continues to adapt and thrive, prove its value and train professional talent to keep pushing the limits, there will always be a strong legitimacy for the profession. That's my hope. Somewhere right now there's a guy developing the LogoCreator 3000 app. Isn't participation great?

1. Eric Husband, interview by the authors, November 5, 2010.

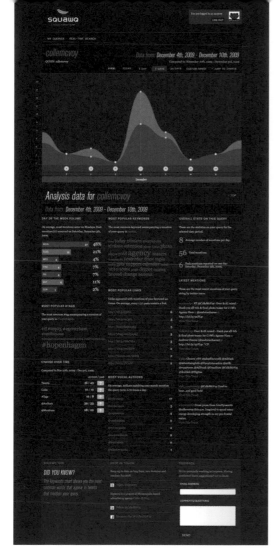

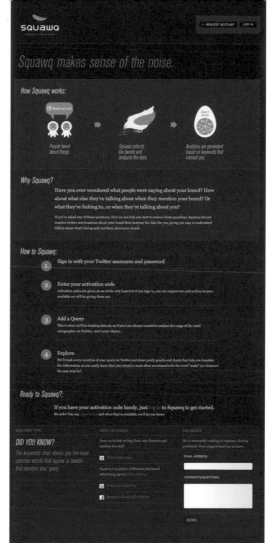

Fig 18 **SQUAWQ**, 2009
www.squawq.com

Colle + McVoy's Squawq collects
Tweets and analyzes the data in
order to monitor how well an ad
campaign is working in the world
of social media. To demonstrate
the new product, the firm analyzed
the Twitter chatter collected during
Super Bowl XLIV in 2009, gathering
sixty-two million media impressions. Squawq ranked the brands
most discussed and provided data
throughout the game.

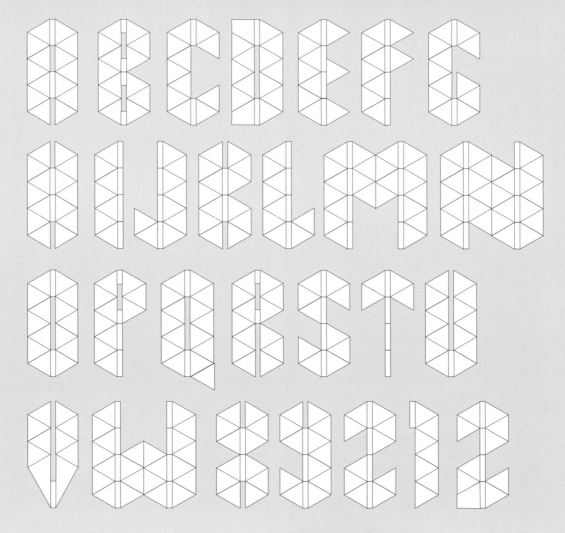

STUDENT WORK: *(above) Elizabeth Beasley, Lindi Biery, Daniel Cha, J. T. Cobell, Greg Cole, Kirsten Gundry, Chris Hurley, Sara Jabbari, Alena Jaffe, Izzy Jarvis, Carla Johnson, Nadia Kabra, Minhee Kim, Harrison Kuykendall, Matt Lewicki, Sarah Straub, Sol Winer, Cameron Wray.*
Graphic Design 1, MICA, fall 2010. FACULTY: Zvezdana Stojmirovic.

STUDENT WORK: *(opposite top) Lindi Biery, Izzy Jarvis. (opposite bottom) Alena Jaffe.*
Graphic Design 1, MICA, fall 2010. FACULTY: Zvezdana Stojmirovic.

TRY THIS PROJECT

Use Google Docs to co-create an alphabet of lettering with a group of participants, working remotely, yet simultaneously, on the same file.

Once your alphabet is complete, use the type to design a poster for a book of your choice. Start by developing three sketches. Consider hierarchy, color, and composition, and balance the co-created lettering with a strong but simple supporting font.

program or be programmed:
ten commandments for a digital age
douglas rushkoff

DOUGLAS RUSHKOFF: *PROGRAM OR BE PROGRAMMED*

On the net, everything is occurring on the same abstracted and universal level. Survival in a purely digital realm— particularly in business —means being able to scale, and winning means being able to move up one level of abstraction beyond everyone else.

we may choose when we wish to live and work in real places, with one another and— unique to living humans —in person

program or be programmed: ten commands for a digital age /douglas rushkoff /or books/new york

Community at Work

GoogleType

Apply existing tools in new and fresh ways by working with the online platform Google Docs. In this two-phased project, MICA students co-created alphabets, working simultaneously on Google Docs documents— text, spreadsheet, or drawing. Once the co-creative stage was completed, each participant downloaded the alphabets and imported them into CS applications as vector-based art. They used the co-created letter-forms to design posters promoting a new book on media theory, *Program or Be Programmed*, by Douglas Rushkoff. In this phase of individual work, students studied composition, color, and hierarchy.

Short Subjects

Harvest available content from the web to develop your own participatory projects. As a graphic designer, you are called to organize, interpret, and lend context to the dizzying troves of data available on the Internet.

In this sophomore project at Montana State University, students used Wikipedia content to design and illustrate standard booklets. Editorial choice became important as they developed public information into unique visual experiences. Shifting from the digital to the physical realm changed the experience of reading from the exposed flatness of the screen to a focused, more intimate, and tactile event. By posting their work back online on the website shortsubjects.info, students underlined the added value of their design.

Design a standard format for a booklet that all participants of the project can use, and set up web space for the digital part of the assignment.

Select a topic on Wikipedia. Carefully read and download the content, before editing it to be more concise and interesting. Illustrate the text to enhance it further and design a booklet using the standard format provided.

Print and bind an edition of five copies of your booklet and number and sign each one. Create a Flash version of your design and upload it to the project website.

STUDENT WORK: *(left) Brian Abbott, Gabrielle Althoff, Alexa Audet, Josh Bock, Brandee Brock, North Bryan, Shaun Cok, Riley Cole, Brittany Constantino, Colton Davies, Samantha Delvo, Kevin Dowsett, Andrew Duchesneau, Ellie Dykstra, Jacob Evans, Dominique Fultz, Chad Green, Lena Haines, Krystle Horton, Bre Huston, Lynlea Jayo, Jessica Jones, Jenny Keller, Casey Kutz, Shay Lee, Jennifer Lister, Andrew Lockhart, Lawson Maclean, Miranda McAdams, Emily Newhouse, Sarah Palecek, Kristie Peck, Jen Pursell, Charlotte Rindos, Andrew Rosenberger, Logan Rovreit, Jesse Shirley, Nikki Simon, Shelby Singleton, Allie Sticka, Ryan Stoll, Aric Tarr, Carly Taylor, Haley Van Heel, Andreas Welch, Will Windham, Skyler Ybarra.*

Form and Content, Montana State University, spring 2010. FACULTY: *Nathan Davis and Jason Johnson, Montana State University.*

Connotations: Search for Content

Celebrate new legal protections that encourage reuse and remixing. The Creative Commons license allows authors to reserve some rights while granting others to the creative public. Learn about the ethical and design principles of sharing.

Students at Montana State University collected images from the photo sharing site Flickr. They posted them on a communal wall, curating clusters of images with similar connotations and exploring image/type relationships. In a gesture of reciprocity, they posted their remixes back to Flickr with a list of credits for all photos used in the project. Under the Creative Commons license the student work was made available to the community.

TRY THIS PROJECT

Open a Flickr account and provide participants with a common physical space where they can display images, such as a wall or board. Collect and crop twenty images from Flickr.

Make sure the pictures are protected by the Creative Commons license. Print and display all images on the image wall or board.

Once all participants have posted their selections, choose any sixteen images from the wall or board that resonate. Assemble them into a square composition and apply a word to activate their content.

Produce a printed mounted version and a digital version. Upload the digital file to the project Flickr account.

STUDENT WORK: *(above) Michael Allport, Megan Baker, Heather Bauer, Andrea Bennyhoff, Claire Carkulis, Amara Crane, Sarah Daniels, Jessica Deily, David Driscoll, Anita Duran, Moriah Ellig, Maxwell Engelmann, Jean-Claude Epskamp, Serena Finn, Nayely Gonzalez, Paul Gorsuch, Metta Hallinan, Haitham Hayat, Anne Heetderks, Diana Heryford, Grayce Holcomb, Barbara Hoscheid, Kellee Kackman, Thor Kanning, Nicole Koning, Christine Lange, Sara Livingston, Jaute Loftin, Casey Lutz, Allie McRae, Ashley Moon, Shane Niederklein, Karinne Noah, Erin Noreen, Jordan Perbil, Shayla Preeshl,*

Jennifer Pursell, Theodore Rindos, Katie Rodriguez, Samuel Rohrich, Nikki Romero, David Runia, Bret Sander, Jacob Sarlo, Candice Schear, Walter Shaw, Kristina Smith, Callie Spencer, Christopher Stanick, Vanessa Swenson, Aric Tarr, Bryce Tiernan, Brittany Tyler, Devan Van Epps, Kylie Walter, Xingchen Wang, Pierce Ware, Carson Wiser, Melissa Zahara, Sam Ziegler.

Design Principles, Montana State University, fall 2010. FACULTY: *Nathan Davis, with help from Meta Newhouse, Jason Johnson, and Ixtla Vaughan, Montana State University.*

Crowdspeak

Workflow—the order in which tasks are undertaken—plays an important role in participatory projects. Explore how workflow can affect authorship and help build community. In this cross-institutional assignment, sophomores at MICA and Miami University pushed the boundaries of authorship. Working with the word *post,* they co-created letterforms by receiving, altering, and passing on files in a digital assembly line. This workflow dislocated authorship from the individual and placed it within the collective, as resultant letterforms aggregated into a final, animated sequence.

TRY THIS PROJECT

Pick a word for your topic and make templates in Adobe Illustrator, establishing the size and placement of each letter. Set up web space, such as a Google Docs account, for file storage.

Divide your group into teams: one team for each letter of the word. Provide the participants with templates and contact lists.

Start an Illustrator file chain. Add a small amount of vector graphics to your template, leaving room for all of the members of your team to contribute. Post a JPG of your file to Google Docs and email the AI file to the next person on your contact list. In turn, you will receive an AI file from the person preceding you on the contact list. Consider its content and add an increment of vector graphics.

Each time you make a contribution, post a JPG of your file to Google Docs before emailing the AI file to the next person. This enables all participants to preview the final piece.

Use only vector graphics and no color. Contribute only small portions and respond thoughtfully to what your peer before you has done.

Once all letters are completed, choose a team of editors to collect all JPG files into one large animated sequence using After Effects.

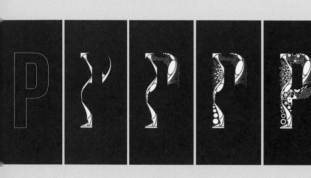

STUDENT WORK: *(top) Krista Adkins, Elizabeth Beasley, Lindi Biery, Adam Cassidy, Daniel Cha, Erika Chitwood, JT Cobell, Greg Cole, Rachael Fraleigh, Reid Groth.*
Graphic Design 1, MICA, *and Typography 1, Miami University, fall 2010.*
FACULTY: *Zvezdana Stojmirovic,* MICA, *and Helen Armstrong, Miami University.*

STUDENT WORK: *(left) Krista Adkins, Elizabeth Beasley, Lindi Biery, Adam Cassidy, Daniel Cha, Erika Chitwood, JT Cobell, Greg Cole, Rachael Fraleigh, Reid Groth, Kirsten Gundry, Paige Hake, Chris Hurley, Julia Hustedt, Sara Jabbari, Alena Jaffe, Izzy Jarvis, Carla Johnson, Nadia Kabra, Minhee Kim, Harrison Kuykendall, Matt Lewicki, Amy Lewin, Jennifer Miller, Marie Mock, Kiera Morgan, Chelsea Nauman, Jenna Samuels, Emily Schwegman, Catherine Scott, Jeremy Smetana, Brittany Stechschulte, Molly Stiebler, Sarah Straub, Eric Villarreal, Sol Winer, Cameron Wray.*
Graphic Design 1, MICA, *and Typography 1, Miami University, fall 2010.*
FACULTY: *Zvezdana Stojmirovic,* MICA, *and Helen Armstrong, Miami University.* SEE BIGGER IMAGE OF THIS PROJECT ON PAGES 2 AND 3.

Community Principles

Co-creation versus Collaboration Co-creation is a new way of working that welcomes user input in the creative process. Participants contribute small parts toward a greater outcome. Co-creation differs from traditional collaboration in that it opens work up to participants outside traditional work settings. Unlike collaboration, co-creation requires a modular work structure. Users contribute modules that help define, shape, and make the product. Co-creation flattens hierarchical orders, as participants both within and outside companies join in problem solving. Ownership is often distributed across the project to everyone involved.

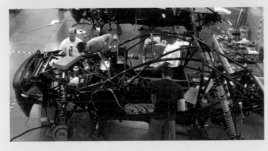

THRILL JOCKEY RECORDS PRESENTS... A POST-PUNK MADLIB!

Double Dagger¹ is playing in _____ on _____
                    CITY   DATE
at a really cool spot called _____. They're
                              VENUE
playing with _____ and
              BAND/PERFORMER/DJ
_____, but not with
BAND/PERFORMER/DJ
_____ unfortunately. I
ALL-TIME FAVORITE BAND
think that this show will be
really _____! I hear that
        ADJECTIVE
there will be _____ girls
              ADJECTIVE
and _____ guys there.
     ADJECTIVE

¹ For more information, _____ Double Dagger.
                        FAVORITE SEARCH ENGINE

Fig 19 **NIKE**, 2008
www.senseworldwide.com/
insightshownike/

(top left) In 2008, working with Sense Worldwide, Nike recruited "cultural experts"—web-savvy trendsetters from key cities in their consumer base—to co-create a brand strategy with community investment. In this example, user input helped build authenticity.

Fig 20 **RALLY FIGHTER**, 2010
www.local-motors.com

(bottom left) In 2009 Local Motors premiered the Rally Fighter, a co-created off-road desert racer that is also street legal. The Rally Fighter design was created by Sangho Kim, a third-year transportation design student. After Kim's design was chosen for production, online community members flocked to design the secondary parts. Featured in the photo are Jay Zuppardo, Zachary Zuppardo, and Brett Zuppardo.

Fig 21 **DOUBLE DAGGER**, 2009
www.posttypography.com

(above) In an example of nondigital participation, Post Typography created Mad Libs posters to promote their band, Double Dagger, inviting the public to fill in the blanks.

"CONTENT IS NOT KING—CONTACT IS."
DOUGLAS RUSHKOFF, *PROGRAM OR BE PROGRAMMED*, 2010

Community Community is an alliance formed along shared interests. Today's digital tools enable us to build communities free from the restrictions of space and time. In the online world, we can become part of social networks by "friending" on Facebook, "digging" on Digg, or "hearting" on Etsy. Community is visualized by the number of approving "hits" to your page, which are available for all to see.

 As consumers with a public voice, online communities are redefining big business. Rather than resisting this shift in power relations, savvy companies encourage online communities to join in the making of products, building strong bonds with their customers. It is precisely this engagement with activated communities in the building of "co-creation experiences" that opens up fresh possibilities for graphic designers.[1]

Community Thinking In a connected culture, community takes over tasks once performed by the individual, including thinking. Need to pick a restaurant? Buy a tool? Learn a craft? Public opinion can easily be accessed online: the number of visits a site gets, and ratings or comments by users can help the decision-making process. The key elements of thinking—reasoning, decision making, and reflection—can now happen with the backing of vast, activated audiences.

 Decisions once made alone or in consultation with immediate associates are increasingly distributed to online communities and digital databases. Inner thought processes are exteriorized. No longer solely the realm of the sovereign body, they are now a participatory activity that can happen across time and space.

1 C. K. Prahalad and
  Venkatram Ramaswamy,
  *The Future of Competition:
  Co-Creating Unique Value with
  Customers* (Boston: Harvard
  Business Press, 2004), 19–34.

"THE INDUSTRIAL AGE CHALLENGED US TO RETHINK THE LIMITS OF
THE HUMAN BODY: WHERE DOES MY BODY END AND THE TOOL BEGIN?
THE DIGITAL AGE CHALLENGES US TO RETHINK THE LIMITS OF THE
HUMAN MIND: WHAT ARE THE BOUNDARIES OF MY COGNITION?"
DOUGLAS RUSHKOFF, *PROGRAM OR BE PROGRAMMED*, 2010

"THE FUNDAMENTAL ACT OF FRIENDSHIP AMONG PROGRAMMERS IS THE SHARING OF PROGRAMS....THE PURCHASER OF SOFTWARE MUST CHOOSE BETWEEN FRIENDSHIP AND OBEYING THE LAW."

RICHARD STALLMAN, "GNU MANIFESTO," 1993

Copyright

Copyright law protects content from being reused without permission. This runs counter to digital culture, which has spawned a generation of remix artists who reassemble bits and pieces of existing works into original formations. These creatives see existing culture as material to be dissected, molded, and shaped into new expressions. They have inspired some of the efforts to democratize copyright law described here.

Copyleft

In the 1980s software activist Richard Stallman proposed the term *copyleft*—all rights reversed—as a rebuttal to the traditional legal label, *copyright*—all rights reserved. Copyleft ensures that a program, or other creative work, will remain free, despite any modifications made to it by volunteer programmers. In 1989 Stallman launched the GNU General Public License, an early legal tool ensuring the long-term freedom of software (www.gnu.org/copyleft).

Creative Commons

Legal scholar Lawrence Lessig founded the free culture movement to promote greater legal freedom in the reuse of published content. In 2001 he helped establish the Creative Commons, a nonprofit organization granting flexible legal licenses that offer a range of legal protections. By 2009 Creative Commons licenses protected over 350 million works (www. creativecommons.org).

Friend, Follower, Fan In recent years, both fandom and celebrity have discovered new, decentralized, independent pathways. With the advent of YouTube and other platforms for homegrown media, people can gain popularity while sidestepping the establishment. Similarly, fans can follow nontraditional modes of celebrity by "friending," "following," or "digging" online content. In doing so they build reputational currency and influence in their online communities.[2] In the digital world, publicizing whom and what you like establishes membership in a community.

Open Source Movement Guided loosely by the nonprofit Open Source Initiative (OSI), the open source movement is a broad coalition of computer programmers who believe in a decentralized, co-creative approach to software development. The guiding principle of open source is that software should remain accessible for improvement by any willing volunteer. A typical open source project involves dozens, even hundreds, of developers working independently on software modules, offering them up for peer review and integration into the larger project. Examples of well-known open source programs include Linux, Apache, MySQL, and PHP. The open source movement presents a useful model and source of inspiration to the design profession, looking to reinvent itself within today's shifting cultural landscape.

2   Chris Anderson, *Free: The Future of a Radical Price* [New York: Hyperion, 2009], 163.

STUDENT WORK: *(below) Design Principles, Montana State University, fall 2010.* FACULTY: *Nathan Davis, with help from Meta Newhouse, Jason Johnson, and Ixtla Vaughan, Montana State University.* SEE PAGE 41 FOR COMPLETE CREDITS.

Participation

By opening up to participants during the phases of ideation, concept development, and strategy planning, designers can become more transparent and build
lasting relationships with activated audiences. Participatory culture allows
them to engage others in their work without the necessity of monetary reward.
Reward can come in other ways, including reputation, acknowledgment, and
reciprocity. Participation can be encouraged in the three ways described below.

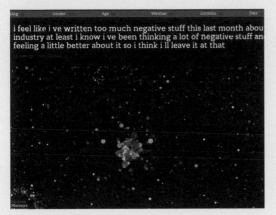

Fig 22 **WE FEEL FINE** 2006
www.wefeelfine.org

The Harvest: Jonathan Harris and Sep Kamvar's We Feel Fine is
a search engine for feelings expressed on the web. By punching in
parameters, users can search for instances of specific feelings pulled
from posts in cyberspace. In this latent form of participation, the
contributor is not directly aware of the act of participating.

Fig 23 **THE SKETCHBOOK PROJECT**, 2010
www.arthousecoop.com

The Open Call: A small payment entitles each user to a blank sketchbook, a theme, and a submission deadline for the Sketchbook Project by
Art House Co-op. Clear directives such as these make taking part in a
project simple and achievable.

Fig 24 **DO US A FLAVOUR**, 2008
www.walkers.co.uk

Long-term Immersion: Walkers, the British snack food brand, sought to
reinvigorate its standing in 2008 with the Do Us a Flavour campaign, in
which online users were asked to develop its next flavor of potato chips.
With over one million entries, the tiered contest used digital media as a
core tool in raising the level of customer investment.

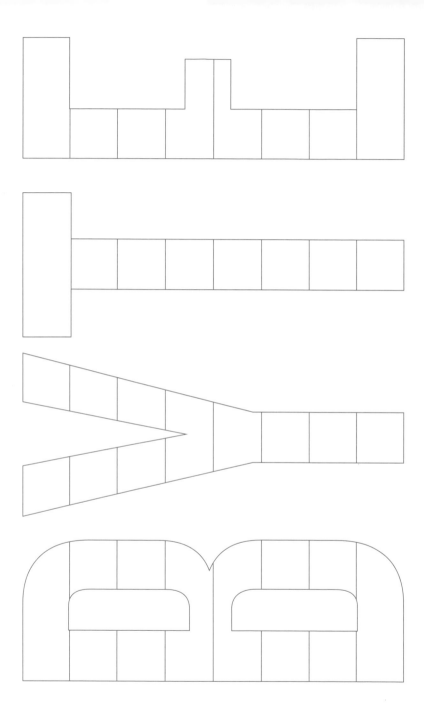

Grab a Byte

Co-create modular letterforms by photocopying this template and then passing it along to a group. This exercise works best with eight participants. Each participant becomes a "bit" of information, filling in one eighth of each of the four letterforms. A byte is a unit of digital information made up of eight bits. Represent digital information by filling in your designated area with simple graphic content, such as hatched lines, a dotted surface, or anything else that might come to mind. When the letterforms are complete, scan them in and enjoy them in digital form.

Modularity

"THE MOST IMPORTANT PART OF A PARTICIPATORY PROJECT IS PROPERLY DESIGNING THE SYSTEM AND TOOLS. THIS IS OBVIOUS, BUT HOW TO GO ABOUT IT ISN'T." AARON KOBLIN, INTERVIEW BY AUTHORS, 2010

In the twenty-first century, design projects can live perpetually in an unfinished state. They can exist as systems of parts that users can construct and customize. Or they can connect thousands of people through large-scale collaborative open-ended undertakings. Modularity makes these living designs possible, breaking up design solutions and processes into systems that embrace rather than compete with activated users.

In general, modularity describes a group of units, or modules, that make up a larger system. Such modules, while structurally independent, still manage to work together.[1] This chapter considers the term in two ways that are particularly apt for the design profession. First, it considers modularity as the formal structure of a multiunit design to which a user can contribute content: a modular system versus a more traditional singular fixed solution. Then it examines modularity as a division of labor used to collaboratively solve a design problem. This approach speaks to the creative process on the decentralized structure of the Internet, which can expand the range of a single project to a multitude of people. Through both approaches, modularity serves as a key to twenty-first-century participatory designs.

Throughout most of the twentieth century, graphic designers provided set results to clients.[2] They created, for example, a poster, a publication, a package, an identity. Modularity can break apart such fixed deliverables, replacing them with more open-ended solutions. Rather than delivering an artifact to a client, designers can supply tools that users can engage. MeBox, a customizable storage system developed by the London-based firm Graphic Thought Facility, puts this idea into action. [Fig 25] Users can press perforated discs out of the carton boxes to create initials, numbers, symbols, and texts. When assembled, the boxes' double-thick construction displays the user's message against a colorful

1 For an extensive discussion of modularity, see Carliss Y. Baldwin and Kim B. Clark, *Design Rules, vol. 1, The Power of Modularity* (Cambridge, Mass.: MIT Press, 2000), 63.

2 For an extensive discussion of twentieth-century design, see Johanna Drucker and Emily McVarish, *Graphic Design History: A Critical Guide* (Upper Saddle River, N.J.: Prentice Hall, 2009).

contrasting lining. To utilize the containers, customers must engage in the boxes' communication system. The design not only encourages participation, it requires it. And it does so in a fun, creative manner.

Stockholm-based designer Mia Cullin also makes use of a modular configuration in her Tyvek textiles Flake and Flower. These products invite users to interlock small units to create rich textures. [Fig 26] Cullin constructs much of her work from set modular units, thereby empowering her customers to complete the production process. Korean designers Min Choi and Sulki Choi employed a similar approach in their promotional materials for the third Women & Spatial Culture Festival in Seoul (2005). This project, titled Toilet Swapping, uses a series of pictograms based on the standard toilet pictogram to investigate the toilet as a gendered space. [Fig 27] Choi and Choi produced these pictograms as a series of stickers that were sent as the event invitation. Attendees could play with the stickers at home or arrange them on displayed promotional posters as a way of exploring the topic both privately and publicly. Such fixed systems of components provide users with easy avenues for participation. As noted by Nina Simon in her recent book about participatory culture and the museum, "The best participatory experiences are not wide open. They are scaffolded to help people feel comfortable engaging in the activity."[3]

While the fixed units of these modular systems make participation manageable, the drawback to this approach is that, although users can rearrange the units in many ways, the formal outcomes are limited. Consider, for example, a system of Legos. The possible formations are many, but the final result will always look like a Lego construction.[4] Each of the modular projects described above maintains a set, distinct look and texture, despite user involvement. Therein lie both the beauty and limitations of modular systems.[5]

Contemporary technology, however, can escape such limitations, making possible systems that are both manageable and flexible. As theorist Lev Manovich points out in his essay "Remixability and Modularity," "If pre-computer modularity leads to repetition and reduction, post-computer modularity can produce unlimited diversity."[6] Manovich looks to a world in which "any

3   Nina Simon, *The Participatory Museum* (Santa Cruz: Museum 2.0, 2010), 13.

4   Lego provides participatory options on its site, including custom kits called Design by Me and a Lego social networking site for sharing work. See http://www.lego.com/en-us/createandshare/default.aspx.

5   For a discussion of modularity and graphic design, see Ellen Lupton and Jennifer Cole Phillips, *Graphic Design The New Basics* (New York: Princeton Architectural Press, 2008), 158–73.

6   Lev Manovich, "Remixability and Modularity," *Lev Manovich* (blog), October–November 2005, http://www.manovich.net/ (accessed November 20, 2010).

"A MODULE IS 'A SCALE OF PROPORTIONS THAT MAKES THE BAD DIFFICULT AND THE GOOD EASY.'" ALBERT EINSTEIN TO LE CORBUSIER, *OEUVRE COMPLETE 1938–46*, 1946

Fig 25 **MEBOX**, 2002
www.graphicthoughtfacility.com

Graphic Thought Facility designed this customizable storage system as a self-initiated project. Users can press out perforated discs from the ends of each box to create initials, numbers, symbols, and texts. When assembled, the double-thick construction presents the message against a contrasting color used in the box lining.

Fig 26 **FLAKE**, 2006
www.miacullin.com

Designed by Mia Cullin and produced by the Finnish company Woodnotes, Flake is a collection of modular star-shaped Tyvek pieces. Users can join these pieces to make three-dimensional curtains or room dividers.

Fig 27 **TOILET SWAPPING**, 2005
www.sulki-min.com

Commissioned by the Feminist
Artist Network, Min Choi and
Sulki Choi developed these
promotional materials for the
third Women & Spatial Culture
Festival in Seoul. The project
invites users to investigate
the toilet as a gendered space.
The main element is a series
of pictogram stickers based on
standard toilet icons. Some of
the stickers were sent out as
invitations so that the recipients
could play with them at home,
while the rest could be freely
applied to the festival poster,
referring to the actual condition
of public toilets in Seoul, usually
covered with colorful stickers.

Fig 28
YEARBOOKYOURSELF, 2009
www.YearbookYourself.com

Colle + McVoy built Yearbook-
Yourself.com for Taubman
Centers, which owns and
operates more than twenty
shopping malls across the
United States. The site lets
children (and parents) upload
photos of themselves to see
what they might have looked
like in different eras, while
learning about the latest mall
fashions. YearbookYourself.com
produced more than thirty
million visitors in the 2008 and
2009 back-to-school seasons,
with each visitor spending an
average of eleven minutes on the
site. Approximately 48 percent
of visitors clicked through to
mall websites, driving traffic
and sales.

well-defined part of any finished cultural object can automatically become a building block for new objects in the same medium. Parts can even 'publish' themselves and other cultural objects can 'subscribe' to them the way you subscribe now to RSS feeds or podcasts." In other words, he envisions a modularity "without a priori defined vocabulary."[7] Indeed, systems are emerging online today that begin to suggest possibilities for a more open kind of modularity. The hard edges of fixed modular units begin to blur as technology enables online modules to dematerialize, user content to blend with preset modules, and a diverse array of users to access the material across systems and devices.

7 Ibid.

Mass Customization

Examples of increasingly open modular systems abound. On sites such as createmychocolate.com (create your own chocolate bars), youbars.com (create your own trail mix), redmoonpetfood.com (create your own pet food), ecreamery.com (create your own ice cream and gelato), and nikeid.nike.com (create custom footwear), users can select specific options from a bevy of preset modules.[8] As opposed to the modularity of the twentieth century, these modules exist as digital options rather than material units. In comparison to, for example, a modular Herman Miller office system of the 1960s, bits translate into physical material only after selections are made. Users create the exact composition and content of modules on the fly, composing the final product as they go. Some companies, such as Jones Soda (custom labels) and Penguin books (custom covers), encourage users to upload their own content, adding an unpredictable element to the overall system. In the past a fixed inventory of premade units limited customers. Today users can customize each module and have the resulting unique item affordably manufactured and delivered, made possible by new fabrication techniques and robotic labor.[9]

8 For discussion of some of these examples and more, see Donald Rattner, "Roundup: Mass Customized Food," *A.R.T. Blog*, http://www.art-rethought.com/blog/2010/07/roundup-mass-customized-food/ (accessed July 8, 2010).

9 For a discussion of new fabrication techniques and customized manufacturing, see Chris Anderson, "In the Next Industrial Revolution, Atoms Are the New Bits," *Wired*, January 25, 2010, http://www.wired.com/magazine/2010/01/ff_newrevolution/ (accessed July 14, 2010).

Consider, for example, blanklabel.com, a custom tailoring site. During the last century, manufacturers slotted clothing into standardized sizes, allowing mass-produced, off-the-rack clothing to flourish. Custom-tailored clothes were

"WITH MODULARITY..., IT IS POSSIBLE TO CHANGE PIECES OF A SYSTEM WITHOUT REDOING THE WHOLE. DESIGNS BECOME FLEXIBLE AND CAPABLE OF EVOLVING AT THE MODULE LEVEL."

CARLISS YOUNG BALDWIN AND KIM B. CLARK, *DESIGN RULES*, 2000

limited to the upper echelon of society. Through the modules provided on blanklabel.com, users can select from various collars, sleeves, fabric, and buttons to design their own shirt, uploading their individual measurements at the end to ensure the perfect fit. Such projects point to an emerging production model called "mass customization."[10] As the name implies, within this model, individual personalization mixes with mass production. Technology and modularity enable the process.

Mass customization can also be found in contemporary graphic design projects. In the past, graphic design has not typically been a one-off process. While our work has always been made according to the specific needs of our clients, it has also usually been mass-produced. It is reproducible, while the mass customization sites described above manufacture unique products for each user. How can the same type of open modularity allow graphic designers to create work that welcomes user input and allows each iteration of a design to vary according to the specific user in question? How can flexible modular systems move to the next level through customization?

Canadian typographer Marian Bantjes's 2007 project for Faber books' new line of one-off, on-demand versions of previously out-of-print books, called Faber Finds, provides one example of modular customization. [Fig 29] Faber books commissioned Bantjes to develop four border patterns based on a custom font designed by Michael C. Place. Each pattern has a distinct personality, as each represents a different literary genre. A team of programmers led by Karsten Schmidt then developed an automated system that breaks the patterns into modules to generate a unique book cover each time a customer orders a book.[11] Bantjes's initial artwork is thus broken apart by technology into customizable modules, which are reconfigured anew for each user. No two copies of the books are alike. In fact, the specific cover imagery for each iteration does not exist until a customer orders it.

Peer Production

In addition to providing a flexible alternative to fixed design solutions, twenty-first-century modularity, with a little help from the Internet, can also restructure the creative process itself. Rather than a single individual or firm working to solve a design problem, imagine a large mass of individuals, each working

10 Stan Davis, *Future Perfect*, 10th anniversary ed. (Reading, Mass.: Addison-Wesley Publishing, 1996); B. Joseph Pine, *Mass Customization: The New Frontier in Business Competition* (Boston: Harvard Business Press, 1993). The concept of mass customization was first conceived by Davis in *Future Perfect* and further developed by Pine in *Mass Customization*.

11 For more on the design side of this project, see Marian Bantjes's website: http://www.bantjes.com/project/faber-finds-borders. For further discussion of the technical side of this project, see the blog PostSpectacular, authored by Karsten Schmidt: http://postspectacular.com/process/20080711_faberfinds-launch.

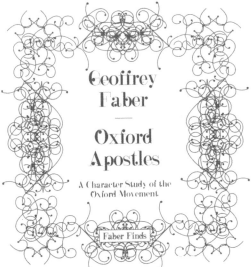

Fig 29 **FABER FINDS**, 2007
www.bantjes.com
www.postspectacular.com

Marian Bantjes designed a
series of borders for the covers
of Faber Finds books, based on a
custom font by Michael C. Place.
Bantjes's series was then used
by Karsten Schmidt to develop a
computer program that generates a unique iteration of the
borders for every cover printed.

Fig 30 **MARKET SQUARE**, 2007
www.brettyasko.com

Commissioned by the Three
Rivers Arts Festival, Pennsylvania,
graphic designer Brett Yasko
created this public art piece for
the Market Square in Pittsburgh.
After spending time in the
square listening to conversations
by passersby, he spelled out
excerpts from these dialogues
in two-foot squares—with each
square holding one letter—near
where the actual words were
spoken. Yasko displayed a different excerpt every other day of the
two-week festival.

Fig 31 **DRIPS**, 2008
www.designercraftsman.com

Designer and metalsmith
Richard Elaver programs
modeling software to generate
forms with random varia-
tions based on simulations of
nature. The resulting forms,
or drips, construct a modular
system. Users can put together
the components to endless
variation.

Rather than following the
traditional path of mass production, Elaver looks to the unique
qualities of nature—the one-
off products of genetic code.
He programs sequences that
produce uniqueness, creating
individualized products for each
user. Drips was a collaboration
with Phil Renato, chair of the
Jewelry Design Program at
Kendall College.

Fig 32 **OSOEX30, THE WAY
WE WORK**, 2006
www.mendedesign.com

In collaboration with the design
firm Volume, MendeDesign
created a participatory campaign
for the San Francisco gallery
Southern Exposure that ques-
tioned the traditional approach
to gallery announcements.
Invitations that doubled as
stencils were mailed out to the
general public. On the invites,
the locations of prehung poster
templates were listed, so recipients could take their stencils
and use them to create unique
designs throughout the city.

The backs of the posters were
designed to easily fold down into
exhibition catalogs. These were
readily available at the show so
attendees could fold and staple
their own document of the entire
experience.

across time and space to solve a bite-sized piece of the same problem. In *The Wealth of Networks*, Benkler describes this kind of emerging production model as "peer production." Modularity, he emphasizes, is key to this new division of labor: "If modules are independent, individual contributors can choose what and when to contribute independently of one another. This maximizes their autonomy and flexibility to define the nature, extent, and timing of their participation in the project."[12]

The distributed, connected nature of the web makes this kind of modularity possible. Projects can be addressed simultaneously by an unlimited number of people using their laptops or mobile devices. This flexible synchronous labor force overturns time as a project constraint. Moreover, each person can work according to his or her individual strength. All participants need not be the same type of skilled worker. Instead, all users benefit from the resulting aggregate brain.[13] This pooling of knowledge manifests in a shared resource, an information commons.

Benkler describes the decentralized nature of peer production and the information commons that supports it as "a new modality of organized production: radically decentralized, collaborative, and non proprietary; based on shared resources and outputs among widely distributed, loosely connected individuals who cooperate without relying on either market signals or managerial commands."[14] The roots of this decentralized modular approach to problem solving lie in the free software movement, begun by Linux founder Stallman in 1985 (see page 14), which encouraged, and still encourages, users to edit and refine a piece of software, allowing them to work on as large or small a section as they wish. In other words, programmers break up software development into manageable modular pieces that allow each participant independence and flexibility. The evolving shared source code provides a commons of knowledge that everyone can learn from and build upon. This kind of collaborative

12 Yochai Benkler, *The Wealth of Networks: How Social Production Transforms Markets and Freedom* (New Haven, Conn.: Yale University Press, 2006, 100. See also chapter 3: "Peer Production and Sharing," 59–90.

13 For an extended discussion of aggregate thinking, see Cass R. Sunstein, *Infotopia: How Many Minds Produce Knowledge* (New York: Oxford University Press, 2006).

14 Benkler, *The Wealth of Networks*, 60.

"IN THE FUTURE ANYONE WILL BE ABLE TO ACCESS VIA THE INTERNET THE MATRIX DESIGN OF A CHAIR, A RADIATOR, OR EVEN A CAR, AND CUSTOMIZE IT.... THIS WILL TRANSFORM DESIGN, PRODUCTION, DISTRIBUTION, AND SHOPPING IN RADICAL WAYS."

PAOLA ANTONELLI, *DESIGN AND THE ELASTIC MIND*, 2008

approach has spread through the world of science and business, leading to significant discoveries.[15] A similarly modular process can be used in visual arts to empower a mass of geographically separated designers to collaborate on a project much bigger than any individual could manage. Striving for an ambitious creative goal, they can work independently, yet within a broad, decentralized team.

To test this concept, my coauthor Zvezdana Stojmirovic and I developed a simple collaborative project called Linked for some of our students at Miami University and MICA in the spring of 2009. We asked fifty-seven students from these two institutions to collaborate on creating letterforms making up the word *linked*, using a modular workflow that we had developed. Each student created a single module, a two-second animation that was then combined with the other modules to create a larger animation, exploring the concept of "linked" in contemporary society.[16] While the work was in process, students could preview the piece publicly on Vimeo, which became a shared creative resource. The project was made possible by existing web tools such as Flickr, Google Docs, and Vimeo. A similar kind of workflow could be applied across a larger number of institutions, between institutions and businesses, or among various design firms, harnessing a decentralized professional creative force or welcoming more wide-ranging user participation. The process could be fit either inside or, preferably, outside existing proprietary structures to produce different types of capital—monetary, promotional, or social.

Data visualization artist Aaron Koblin develops a wide range of peer production projects constructed of modular workflows. Many of his pieces utilize Amazon's Mechanical Turk site (www.mturk.com/mturk), a distributed labor tool that allows users to complete small modules of larger projects in exchange for micropayments. Mechanical Turk thus granulates human labor and suggests new possibilities for multiple microrevenue streams.

15 For a discussion of companies using a crowdsourcing approach, see Don Tapsoctt and Anthony D. Williams, *Wikinomics: How Mass Collaboration Changes Everything* (New York: Portfolio, 2006); see also Jeff Howe, *Crowdsourcing: Why the Power of the Crowd Is Driving the Future of Business* (New York: Crown Business, 2008).

16 For an extensive discussion of Linked, see page 77.

"THE TOOLS OF FACTORY PRODUCTION, FROM ELECTRONICS ASSEMBLY TO 3-D PRINTING, ARE NOW AVAILABLE TO INDIVIDUALS, IN BATCHES AS SMALL AS A SINGLE UNIT."

CHRIS ANDERSON, *WIRED*, JANUARY 2010

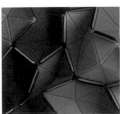

Fig 39 **CLOUDS**, 2008
www.bouroullec.com
www.kvadratclouds.com

Industrial designers Ronan &
Erwan Bouroullec developed
this new textile tile concept in
collaboration with the textile
company Kvadrat. The modular
tiles, connected by special rubber
bands, can be combined as an
installation or hung from a wall
or ceiling.

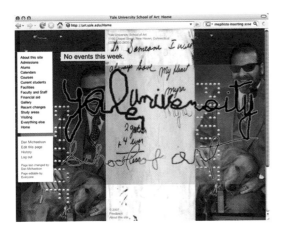

Fig 40 **YALE UNIVERSITY
SCHOOL OF ART WEBSITE**, 2006
www.blog.linkedbyair.net
www.art.yale.edu

Tamara Maletic and Dan
Michaelson, of the New York
graphic design partnership
Linked by Air, developed Yale
University's School of Art website
as a new kind of modular wiki.
They designed the site to be fed by
content from the students, staff,
and faculty of the school, creating
a modular workflow that replaced
top-down content creation.

Koblin's projects include the Bicycle Built for Two Thousand (voice recordings collected from 2,088 online workers and then assembled into the song "Daisy Bell," www.bicyclebuiltfortwothousand.com), Ten Thousand Cents (a drawing of a hundred dollar bill created by thousands of individuals working in isolation from one another) [Fig 39], and The Johnny Cash Project (drawings by participants that are woven into a collective tribute to Johnny Cash, set to his song "Ain't No Grave"). [Fig 37] When thousands of strangers collaborate on a visual project, the results, as in Koblin's work, can be quite stunning. While using the labor of others, the artist plays a key role in each of these projects. Without his original concept, his system for dividing the work into enticing manageable bits, his promotion of the overall project, and the ultimate compilation, none of these pieces would come to fruition. Creative professionals such as Koblin suggest a provocative role for the designer in the world of participation: that of a leader, an educator, who enables the work of others, elevating their creations by contextualizing them within a larger goal. He is, in a sense, the creative director of a decentralized, largely untrained workforce.

Amsterdam-based designer Jonathan Puckey also utilizes a modular structure for his large-scale collaborative work. Together with designer and director Roel Wouters, he created a crowdsourced music video for the musicians C-Mon & Kypski called One Frame of Fame. [Fig 35] The site developed for the project asks users to photograph themselves mimicking poses demonstrated by the musicians. Each hour the video updates with new user contributions, weaving the photos into the overall video, which is perpetually remaking itself.

Cameron Sinclair's organization Architecture for Humanity experiments with a peer-to-peer collaborative model on a larger scale. On his site, openarchitecturenetwork.org, architects, designers, builders, and their clients can upload architectural plans and drawings—including CAD files—addressing the issue of affordable housing for slum dwellers. The structure of the site is modular, decentralized, and nonproprietary. Participants share ideas through an open source model, making their work freely downloadable. Through this shared resource of architectural plans and concepts, users can collaboratively begin to solve the organization's overarching goal of "improvement in the lives of 100 million slum dwellers by the year 2015."[17] No one individual vision

17 This is the UN Millennium Development Goal. The Open Architecture Network hopes to achieve it by 2015. See the Open Architecture Network site: http://openarchitecturenetwork.org/about.

directs the projects on the site; instead they grow organically, as multiple smaller projects interact with one another, all drawing on the architectural commons at the core of the site.

Participants here profit not only from the rewarding experience of improving humanity, but also from establishing strong networks with other creatives, raising their own social profile and putting into practice skills that they might otherwise not be able to apply in real world projects. The key to the success of the organization lies in the Creative Commons license, which enables participants to share their work freely, while protecting their intellectual property rights and safeguarding their work from unwarranted for-profit uses. In this way, Architecture for Humanity manages to help those in real need, while not devaluing the work of professional architects. Under the distributed umbrella of Architecture for Humanity, hundreds of collaborative architectural projects develop using the shared resources of the site.

In contrast to the projects described above, sites such as crowdspring.com and 99designs.com show that the participatory strategy of crowdsourcing can also be exploited by clients to the detriment of designers. These sites seek design solutions from large groups of people, but do not engage in modular systems of collaboration. Clients post briefs, including a set fee, and then ask interested users to post possible design solutions. In the end, only one participant is paid, and paid well below market value, for each project. The sites do not encourage collaboration between designers, and there is little communication between designers and clients. Uploads produce no shared resource—no commons—to benefit the larger design community. Rather than a Creative Commons licensing model, old-style proprietary rights are reinforced as the chosen designs are passed on as client property. Such sites pit crowdsourcing participants against the professional design community, devaluing professional work by reducing design to an anonymous commodity. In fact, many find these sites unethical and exploitative.[18]

18 For an interesting discussion of crowdspring.com, see Bob Garfield, an interview with Matt Samson, "The Crowdsourcing Dilemma," On The Media website, July 9, 2010, http://www.onthemedia.org/transcripts/2010/07/09/06 (accessed November 20, 2010); see also Christopher Steiner Forbes, "The Creativity of Crowds," *Forbes Magazine*, January 22, 2009, http://www.forbes.com/forbes/2009/0216/062.html (accessed July 14, 2010).

See the NoSpec Movement: http://www.no-spec.com/.

"IF YOU GIVE STUFF AWAY FOR FREE, IT BECOMES MORE ABOUT YOUR REPUTATION, THE TYPE OF WORK YOU DO, AND HOW MANY PEOPLE CAN ACCESS THAT WORK." KARSTEN SCHMIDT, LECTURE AT GRAPHIC DESIGN FESTIVAL BREDA, 2010

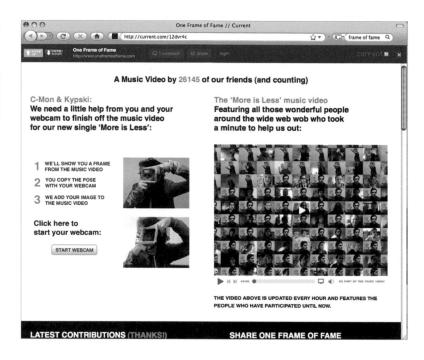

Fig 35 **ONE FRAME OF FAME**, 2010
www.jonathanpuckey.com
www.oneframeoffame.com

Jonathan Puckey designed this crowdsourced music video for the Dutch band C-Mon & Kypski in collaboration with Roel Wouters. On the project website users can follow Puckey's instructions for generating images for the video. They then submit their images and watch as each hour the video updates with new contributions.

Fig 36 **THE SHEEP MARKET**, 2006
www.aaronkoblin.com
www.thesheepmarket.com

For this project, artist Aaron Koblin hired thousands of people through Amazon's Mechanical Turk tool. Each worker was paid two cents to draw a sheep facing to the left. Koblin selected ten thousand sheep for the final collaborative project and posted animations of each sheep's creation on the project website.

The Sheep Market

More fruitful collaborative models lie in the projects described earlier, which reward all of the users involved: Professionals benefit as they establish new niche roles as creative leaders of large decentralized forces, or as they develop previously untapped resources for creative networks, social capital, and larger meaning in their work. Amateur participants benefit from micropayments, public exposure, the establishment of their own creative networks, and the sheer joy of being part of a larger collaborative endeavor. This more open source approach benefits society at large as it promotes a general democratization of communication.

Modularity Invites Participation

Modularity as a design concept based on repetition and reduction became popular during the mid to latter part of the twentieth century. Today, it is being reborn to answer the open call of participatory culture. Through modular systems designers can shake up the fixed solutions of the past, welcoming user involvement. Technology continues to enable them to work with increasingly flexible modules that allow for customization and transformation. Through this new modularity designers can realize fresh, unexpected, generative design solutions.

Modularity can also reconstitute the design process itself. Within the evolving method of peer production, modularity operates as a key organizing structure, providing the independence and flexibility necessary for designers and users to work collaboratively across time and space. Current experiments with such structures hint at revolutionary new types of work that are no longer limited by the hours in the day or the number of workers in an office.

Both as a direction for new types of generative work and as a feasible large-scale collaborative model, modularity invites participation. And, that, as we have seen, can change everything, particularly for the designer.

"I DESIGN THE ENVIRONMENT...AND THEN ALLOW SOMETHING TO GROW WITHIN IT. I FIRST STARTED DOING THIS BY CREATING GRAPHIC DESIGN TOOLS AND THEN WORKING WITH THEM. LATER I STARTED CREATING PROJECTS THAT PARTICIPANTS THEN FINISH." JONATHAN PUCKEY, INTERVIEW BY AUTHORS, 2010

AARON KOBLIN

www.aaronkoblin.com

Artist Aaron Koblin specializes in data visualization and collaborative art making. Currently he leads the Data Arts Team in Google's Creative Lab. Koblin generates open-ended projects, often modular in structure, that are fed by harnessed or voluntarily contributed data. He argues that traditional media for art are far more restrictive than digital technology, suggesting that "creating computer software is the closest we can get to pure mental creation—second perhaps only to creative writing."

Which project first shifted your focus from finished artifacts to open-ended collaborative projects?

Two moments come to mind. The first is the moment I became interested in collaborative art making: the release of Amazon's Mechanical Turk. The Turk, a web service, enables individuals or companies to employ thousands of people on tasks of which they have no context. I asked thousands to draw a picture of a sheep and collected them. This project, the Sheep Market, did have a finite end, though. [Fig 36] I chose to collect ten thousand and the task was specifically designed. The second moment is more applicable: the decision to make the Johnny Cash Project. [Fig 37] This more "open-ended" collaboration continues to accept images of the late music legend. Here each participant understands what he or she is participating in.

How do you incorporate modularity in your work?

Modularity is fundamental to working with large groups of people. When tasks are broken down into discreet steps and tools are assembled into specific components, this allows for a system of scale.

Computers fascinate me because of their ability to turn simple instructions into complex and massive results through iteration and speedy management. In my work I create simple systems of bundling and assembling complex user content to create something bigger than the sum of its parts.

Why do people get involved in your projects?

This varies on a per-project basis. Many were driven by the financial incentive (as minimal as it was) with the Mechanical Turk. Largely, it was also curiosity. Newer projects, such as Johnny Cash, are more about participating in something bigger and taking credit for something well executed. There is amazing reward for being able to put your name on something.

What's the most interesting tech tool or platform that you've seen recently?

I'm excited about some of the open standards being rolled into web browsers. Things like Canvas when combined with JavaScript and socket connections open up a world of possibilities for creative collaboration. We're just at the tip of the iceberg, thinking about how to use these powerful tools for visualization, UI, and collaborative creation.

Which three artists do you think are currently doing intriguing work?

Golan Levin may always be one of my favorite artists. His ability to turn a machine into something human and intimate inspired me to get into whatever it is that I do. Many of his students have also gone on to do interesting things. Zach Lieberman's work is equally inspiring, both as an artist and as leader of an open source tools library. Finally, I would say Ben Fry, who has consistently created beautiful and meaningful data-driven work, as well as developing the bulk of the Processing programming language that enabled me to get somewhere with software.

Describe your role in a collaborative work such as the Sheep Market. If other people are supplying the content, what are you doing as an artist?

I've heard people compare my process to that of the Fluxus artists—creating a series of rules and instructions followed by others. Ultimately, it's creating a system, an algorithm executed in part by technology and in part by humans. I'm conducting an interplay between components, managing perceptions, requests, constraints, and assembly.

How do you negotiate the loss of control that comes with opening work to unpredictable users?

For different projects I have done this to greater/lesser extents. For each there are "sweet spots" based on intersections of procedural decisions. Each decision brings a different narrative. I'm always conscious of this. What does the project method say? How are the contributions affected by these choices? What does that say about the entire process?

I like to work on projects greater than myself, where it's as much a new experience for me as everyone else. While I can affect it, I can't control it.

Many artists and designers shy away from technology, thinking it impedes creativity. What is your position?

I don't think they do. They may not realize they are embracing technology, but everyone is. Many artists prefer the complexity of being in their heads than in their tools, such as painters and sculptors. This, too, is technology, though, and the significance is not that relevant to me. I flourish with constraints and attempt to rebuild them within technology. I would argue that

traditional mediums are in fact far more constraining than high-tech. But this is not perceived, because of the barriers to understanding the complexity. It's for this reason that I've been enamored by open source libraries like Processing, Open Frameworks, etc., which remove some barriers while keeping intact the ability to dig deep and remold the technology to one's own desires. To take this idea further, I might argue that creating computer software is the closest we can get to pure mental creation—second perhaps only to creative writing.

Can you speak to the way technology and craft merge through participatory projects?

This follows the same thread as the previous question: the distinction is perhaps not so significant. There is a point where digital technology is able to achieve such speed and resolution that for all intents and purposes it could be considered analog (and perhaps the reverse is true as well). I'm interested in how ideas can move between mediums and express themselves in different forms.

Have any of your participatory projects been failures?

In Ten Thousand Cents, Takashi [Kawashima] and I were interested in representing the system honestly, employing little moderation, and seeing how well thousands of people would re-create a hundred dollar bill. There were failures within the bill, but mostly it worked. The system did what it was designed to do; the humanity showed through. The most important part of a participatory project is properly designing the system and tools.

This is obvious, but how to go about it isn't. At Google, engineers learned that the best process of designing systems and tools was through an iterative process of testing assumptions—this works well when possible. When it's not, be prepared for chaos and unexpected results, but after all, that's half the fun of it.

THE JOHNNY CASH PROJECT

Explore   Contribute   About | Credits

A UNIQUE
COMMUNAL
WORK,
A LIVING
PORTRAIT
OF THE
MAN
IN
BLACK

Through this interactive
website, participants may
draw their own portrait of
Johnny Cash to be integrated
into a collective whole. As
people all over the world
contribute, the project will
continue to evolve and grow,
one frame at a time.

Submit your drawing to
become a part of the new
music video for the song "Ain't
No Grave". Strung together
and relayed in sequence your
art, paired with Johnny's
haunting song, will become a
living, moving, and ever-
changing portrait of the
legendary Man in Black.

WATCH THE VIDEO

CONTRIBUTE

AARON KOBLIN

Fig 37 **THE JOHNNY CASH PROJECT**, 2009
www.thejohnnycashproject.com

(opposite) In this collaboration with director Chris Milk, Koblin asks each participant to draw one frame from a video set to Johnny Cash's song "Ain't No Grave." Koblin's interactive piece weaves together all of the contributions into one big living, growing tribute to Cash. According to Koblin, the project "represents Cash's continued existence, even after his death, through his music and his fans."[1] By April of 2010, fans had contributed 4,600 frames.

1. Aaron Koblin, "The Johnny Cash Project," Aaron Koblin website, www.aaronkoblin. com/ (accessed November 20, 2010).

Fig 38 **THE WILDERNESS DOWNTOWN**, 2010
www.thewildernessdowntown.com

(above) Koblin collaborated with Google's Creative Lab and Chris Milk to create this interactive HTML5 short. Users can upload the address of the home they grew up in and then watch as the short's protagonist runs down past their childhood home. The piece is set to Arcade Fire's song "We Used to Wait" and was designed to use modern web technologies in Google's Chrome browser.

Fig 39 **TEN THOUSAND CENTS**, 2008
www.tenthousandcents.com

(below) Koblin teamed up with designer and media artist Takashi Kawashima for this collaborative project. Koblin hired thousands of individuals using Amazon's Mechanical Turk tool, paying them one cent apiece to use a custom drawing tool to create a tiny part of a hundred dollar bill. As opposed to the Johnny Cash Project, where participants understand the context of their contribution, individuals worked alone with no knowledge of the purpose behind their labor. All of the drawings come together in a final interactive piece on the project website. With Ten Thousand Cents, Koblin explores new digital labor markets.

JONATHAN PUCKEY

www.jonathanpuckey.com

Jonathan Puckey crafts his own design tools and then works with these custom tools toward unexpected results, allowing the process of making to define his design direction. As Puckey explains, "I want tools to influence the way I work, and I want that to happen in interesting ways." This focus on process, as well as his own impressive programming skills, characterizes much of Puckey's work. He draws inspiration from weekly meetings with Luna Maurer, Edo Paulus, and Roel Wouters. Together they form the Amsterdam-based collective Conditional Design. Here, in miniworkshops, they "create an environment, and then...see what can happen within it."

What is it about big collaborative projects, such as Frame of Fame and Take a Bow, that interests you?

It's part of a larger interest in creating work that isn't finished when it's finished. I design the environment, present the environment, and then allow something to grow within it. I first started doing this by creating my own graphic design tools and then working with them. Later I started creating projects that participants then finish. These participants act within the work. That fascinates me.

What is it like to develop a participatory project and then put it out there?

When you put something out there, you depend on other people to finish it. But they might not be interested in doing this. That was true for Frame of Fame. [Fig 35] We needed 1,400 people to participate. I spent sleepless nights worrying that this was not going to happen. The funny thing was, it happened without any problem. In the first day we had 2,000 participants.

With our latest project, Take a Bow, I had the idea that we would just launch it and everything would be fine. Everyone would do it. But it didn't happen that quickly. It took a couple of days to start spreading.

You are never sure if something's going to work or not. You have to be ready, because whatever comes will be unexpected. This unpredictability is nice. After you design a book, the printed book is never more than you expect it to be. You tend to find mistakes. You're connected to the object you created, but it is never going to become more than that. I enjoy creating projects that I can't control completely.

I had a conversation with Luna a long time ago about the idea of losing control. She said it's not about losing ownership; the ownership just shifts. You choose which part of the project to leave open for the external process, and you design the parameters that this external input will work within. Then you find out how people actually interact with your system, how they both use and fight against the limitations you set for them. These are all useful details that happen after you deliver your project. You can't control it anymore. The things that can happen are exciting.

What do humans bring to the project that you can't program?

For a long time there's been this fascination with the idea that the machine itself will create something. As a programmer you just program something and these amazing random things come out of it. I never believed in that. I believe that technology is nothing without input. People are always a part of what I'm doing with technology. For me, it's a logical way to work.

Is your training in graphic design?
Yes. I was on the losing end of the dot-com wave. The moment I decided to join in, everything crashed. I had a nice month and then was lost for a while. I ended up working at terrible interaction design agencies doing uninteresting work.

Then I decided to study again. I went to the [Gerrit] Rietveld Academie in Amsterdam. They offer a graphic design course that focuses on print design. Previously I had only been working with technology. Print design offered an interesting problem for me, because it results in a static final product—a book, for example. In print design, you have to focus on the making process. An interactive site is measured by how it's being used by people. After a while, I combined my fascination for programming, code, and generative systems with this idea of creating a product that needs to be printed in the end. That was a good limitation for me.

Do you feel that you are still working in that direction, or have you moved away from print recently?
Because I can do everything, I like the idea of staying an amateur in all these little things. I can make, for example, a video clip. Or create a type page, design a book or a website, or I can make a performance, or all of these things. I'm not interested in the details of these. I try to keep it a bit more general.

Your work combines craft and technology through the development of tools, Scriptographer tools, for example. Can you speak to that a little bit?
When I started studying graphic design, I was frustrated by the software. As designers we all work with the same software, mainly Adobe applications. These applications solve the problem of graphic design well. That frustrates me. Standard tools lead us in specific directions, because they only offer certain possibili-

ties. It seems strange that we accept the restrictions that companies offer us. If we accept a computer as a tool, it should be as a way of making our own tools.

Can you give an example of a project that illustrates that?
I made a tool in 2008 called the Delaunay Raster. [Fig 41] I made it not for a specific project; instead, I had this idea about image abstraction, and I wanted to play around with it. The funny thing was that by creating this tool, I generated future projects. People came to me and wanted to work with it. It turned around the standard way of working. Normally you create a project and then someone sees it and wants you to do another similar project. This time, I created a tool, people liked the idea of the tool, and they wanted me to use it for their projects.

Do you think design education should empower designers more to build their own tools? Right now, at least in the United States, undergraduate design departments teach students how to use programs.
It's a complicated thing, because right now you have to really know how to program. I teach programming. We do two workshops a year and we do Scriptographer workshops at ECAL/University [of Art and Design Lausanne] in Switzerland. It's important that people have a notion of what it means to make your own tools. The programming aspect of that I find complicated, because a programmer is a certain type of person. You need to be a bit of a geek.

Are you a little bit of a geek?
Yes, for sure.

What does that mean? What do you have to do?
You have to spend a lot of time. It's becoming easier by the year, but you still have to be able to fail two

hundred times a day. And it's always your fault. There is no leeway. When you are instructing the computer, you have to tell the computer exactly what to do. It demands a precise voice. You have to develop this.

I also teach interactive design at the Rietveld Academie. We don't teach code there, but we try to teach a way of thinking. Instead of asking students to create a static end result, we ask them to create a series of things. The differences in these series are interesting instead of the objects themselves. Instead of programming their own tools, we have them research pieces of software that normally wouldn't be used for graphic design and use them in different ways. This is more of an introduction to how this thinking could change their process. Maybe through that we can interest them in learning to write code, instead of just throwing people into the world of programming.

On the other hand, we also teach Scriptographer at the ECAL, and I'm always impressed in what we can do in a week. I had a workshop last week with forty-two students. I went away thinking that they had an idea of what programming is. We teach them vector geometry and all kinds of crazy things. They seem to be able to take it in and do things with it.

One of the interesting things for me about Scriptographer is that there is this nice relationship with the design environment. You are creating design tools, but you can still manipulate the resulting object within Illustrator, so you can use it in your documents easily. It's a nice balance between working as a designer and working as a programmer; it's almost a 50/50 thing.

How do your weekly Conditional Design collaborations feed your process?

We created these minimeetings because we all shared something within our work. We had never before defined what we shared. We are surrounded by a print design culture in Amsterdam, and we felt like

outsiders in this. We thought it would be nice to write down what defines us and have a conversation around this subject. We wanted to take away, for example, the focus on technology.

Often people speak about our work as generative design or code art. For us, it's not about that. We use technology as part of our work, but actually the focus is the process. We set things in motion, or we create an environment, and then we see what can happen within it. We got together every Tuesday evening for a few months, the four of us at Luna Maurer's kitchen table.

These meetings were important to me because, after graduating from the Rietveld Academie, I felt a complete lack of discussion in my work. You go from discussing your work with your fellow students and teachers, to being in your studio and asking your friends what they think. They say the work's nice. No one has a critical opinion. I felt it was important to create a space to be honest and invest in each other. That became the Conditional Design evenings.

After writing our manifesto, we decided to use these evenings to create work. Through these workshops, we could define better what we were trying to talk about. Every week one of us had to come up with an idea, and then within that evening we had to do it. We built a system where we could document it easily and present it to the outside world directly. Both the failures and successes of the evenings were sent to the outside world.

It was difficult to keep this going. Even though we are still working on things, we are having a two-month break right now and then we'll get back to doing workshops. Quickly after starting the workshops, we began getting questions about exhibitions. Then somehow we started becoming professional with this space, which was meant to be an amateur place where we could just play around. We are trying to find a balance right now.

JONATHAN PUCKEY

Fig 40 **IDENTITY FOR THE BEACH**, 2007
www.jonathanpuckey.com

For The Beach, a new network
organization, Puckey and Stockholm-
based graphic designer Peter Ström
created an identity that feels like a
living organism. They drew each
element of the identity by hand using
Puckey's Tile Tool as an assistive
device. The resulting identity is flexible;
it can evolve and adapt each time
it is applied.

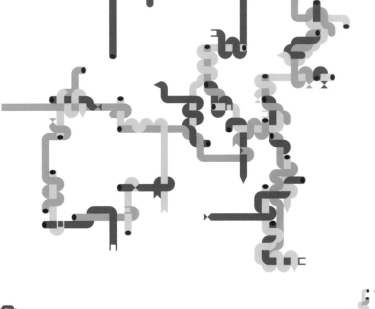

JONATHAN PUCKEY

Fig 41 **DELAUNAY RASTER**, 2008
www.jonathanpuckey.com

(opposite) Puckey developed the
Delaunay Raster to assist in image
vectorization using Scriptographer
and Color Averaging by Jürg Lehni.

Fig 42 **TILE TOOL**, 2006
www.jonathanpuckey.com

(right) For the new record label
Special Box, Puckey created
this typography generated by his
Scriptographer tool, Tile Tool. The
piece is a best-of compilation of
designs created with Tile Tool.

MIA CULLIN

www.miacullin.com

Mia Cullin works as a freelance designer and interior architect in Sweden. Her work with assembled modules reveals an attraction to geometry. She says of modularity: "I am fascinated by the transformation that occurs when objects or shapes are repeated to create different shapes, surfaces, or even functions."

Describe one of your projects that incorporate audience participation.

Two product examples are Flake [Fig 26] and Flower, produced by the Finnish company Woodnotes. The consumer assembles elements in Tyvek (one package consists of 160 pieces) into a room divider or a curtain. It is also possible to create three-dimensional objects. The final size depends on how dense it is assembled, as it is possible to create holes. The finished piece can range from two and a half to four square meters. I like the idea that the consumer can make the final choice. But it depends, of course, on the project!

How are the roles of designer and consumer changing as a result of new manufacturing technologies?

This is interesting. When production methods became available for consumers, anyone could test her ideas. Some people now consider designers to be not necessary: "Anyone can be a designer." This leads to bad products and copies. On the other hand, these possibilities can lead to unique pieces and limited editions of high quality.

Why, in Flake, did you shift your focus from finished artifact to open-ended modular project?

I had already designed that module in a smaller version and used it for "closed" shapes, for example, cushion covers. I found it perfect to enlarge and use for spaces with no fixed measures. The height and width of the room does not matter, as you can assemble as many modules as you like.

What is the most interesting design conversation that you have had recently?

I have just started to work on children's products for a company. The conversation was: What is good design when it comes to children's products? Is it all about security and function?

What role do repetition and granularity play in your work?

It is important for my design. When I work with a product I often think: How will this appear if it is repeated? Should it be possible to make connections? Should it be a part of a system? Is it okay for the consumer to assemble the product by herself?

How can designers avoid being overwhelmed by the constant emergence of new technologies?

It must be a matter of priority. I suppose that if you are really interested in all the novelties, it would be hard. Just because something is new, does it have to be interesting and useful? I must admit that I often work with low-tech design, so it is not a problem for me.

What software programs do you use most?

AutoCAD and Rhino.

What three websites do you visit most frequently?

My webmail, the site of my children's school, and Facebook.

TAMARA MALETIC AND DAN MICHAELSON

www.blog.linkedbyair.net

Tamara Maletic and Dan Michaelson form the graphic design partnership Linked by Air. Their studio divides between technology and design by using systematic digital approaches in their print and environmental projects. Maletic and Michaelson see all of their work as civic space within which users participate, creating their own traffic patterns. In 2006 they developed a website for the Yale University School of Art [Fig 34] built on a modular wiki to be populated not by the administration but, instead, by all members of the school community.

What was it like setting up an open-ended framework for the Yale University School of Art website?

Dan Our concept for the site was that every student, staff, and faculty member should be able to edit every page. On a social level, we observed that students given this responsibility understood that it didn't have to be that way—and it usually wasn't. As a result, they were responsible.

Interestingly, in the first year or two of the site, students made funny pages that used the trappings of official language. For example, they made a page called "Office Hours," in which a student offered advice upon request. They tried to blur the boundary between themselves and the administration of the school. They were engaging with the site in an active critical way.

Tamara The students' quick adjustment to the open structure of the site was not so unexpected. But it surprised me how quickly the staff got into it. They started putting up family photos, pictures of their cats, etc. They also were quickly active in changing the home page and, later on, moved to other sections of the site. That was nice to see.

Has a modular approach bled over from websites into some of your other nondigital projects?

T We explored modularity in the 365 exhibition that we did for the AIGA in 2010. We designed basic furniture that worked as modular containers for content—platforms, magnetic boards, shelves, trollies. These containers encouraged users to browse the works and move them around.

D That project was a literal three-dimensional manifestation of how we had been working on websites. Our presentation at 365 included diagrams of how people interacted with the exhibition. An interest of ours is seeing our work as civic spaces that can be considered in terms of traffic patterns.

How did people react to the AIGA exhibition?

T The magnetic boards where the posters were displayed changed all the time. People put new things on the top layer or moved things around. The platform was constantly rearranged, because it was a pile of things. Some projects would resurface, moving to the top, then later sinking to the bottom. Each person could see a trace of other people experiencing the pieces. People interacted with the work in a casual, not precious, way as they rummaged through this pile.

On opening night people interacted with the work and one another. To complement the show, AIGA provided wireless access in their office for a few months. Also, while the exhibition was up, the receptionist played her iPod on the main speakers. The AIGA was so happy with the exhibition, they kept it up a few extra months. People would stop by and linger in the inviting communal space.

Modularity at Work

Sustain Yourself

Try modular work methods by co-creating a book. In this project, students at MICA worked together to create and publish a book using an on-demand printing service. Working with a greater theme, in this case *sustainability*, can help cohere multifaceted projects. The students' initial task was to make a useful object and hand-cut letterforms out of discarded materials. By documenting their process, the students each created content for one chapter of the book. The chapters were then assembled into one file and printed on Lulu.

TRY THIS PROJECT

Pick a theme.

Engage a team of participants to develop a sample chapter, creating a master InDesign document with pagination and a template for the group to use.

Charge each member of the group to develop content for one chapter of the book.

Give guidance as members start designing their chapters using the template provided. Save them as pdfs.

Import all pdfs into the InDesign master document and publish the book using an on-demand printer.

STUDENT WORK: *(above) Emma Albuquerque, Sean Barrett, Benjamin Belt, Gregory Cole, Meredith Cole, Wendy Du, Colleen Farr, Cassie Johnson, Garrett Lee, Jianna Lieberman, Kirk Liu, Mier Luo, Jasmine Nones-Newman, Barbara Ozieblo, Sol Winer.*

Introduction to Graphic Design, MICA, *spring 2010.* FACULTY: *Zvezdana Stojmirovic.*

Linked

Explore the give-and-take of control, an important aspect of co-creation. A modular workflow is ideal for typographic experiments that cohere a variety of solutions. The right balance between individual integrity and collective authorship helps ensure a rewarding experience for participants. Retaining control over one's own module helps build investment in the whole project. The co-created outcome, however, should appear greater than each individual contribution.

The word *linked* was used as both the topic and the content of this cross-institutional experiment at MICA and Miami University. Each student was asked to contribute an animated module to a final motion graphic of the word.

STUDENT WORK: *(below)* Brianna Antonaccio, Allison Backovski, Amy Baker, Melissa Barat, Megan Barber, Haley Biel, Leigh Bornhorst, Lisa Burn, Kris Carlson, Jason Carter, Shannon Craver, Carey Chiaia, Cherlyn Chong, Alexandra Coyle, Ellen Culpepper, Emily Drumm, Alyse Eversole, Nathalie Garfinkle, Greg Gazdowicz, Victoria Gregory, Meghann Harris, Shannon Hovick, Jinghang Huang, Kara Isabella, Robin Jerome, Coco Kao, Zoe Keller, Katrina Kelly, Erin Killinger, Jihad Kimmey, Sabrina Kogan, Arianne Krekeler, Huong Le, John Lyons, Molly Mackin, Colin McSteen, Nhi Nguyen,

TRY THIS PROJECT

Chose a word as your theme and create an outline template in Illustrator. Set the final pixel dimensions of the motion graphic, as well as the size and placement of each letter module.

Assign a team of participants for each letter.

Give each participant a letter template, and ask him or her to make a two-second motion sequence of that letter. Participants must keep the fixed size of their module, and the letter must start and end in the position indicated on the template.

When all letters are completed, edit them in After Effects to create one large animated piece. Add original, student-created sound.

Colin Nyborg, Seri Park, Kailie Parrish, Dustin Pearce, Jennifer Rezac, Lauren Romano, Joseph Skilton, Alexander Sloves, John Sperandeo, Nathan Tavel, Derek Torsani, Ruth Tsang, Garrett Varady, Jason Walters, Kristen Whaley, Carolyn Williams, Kristen Yagley, Colleen Yates.

Graphic Design 4, MICA, and Design, Perception and Audience, Miami University, spring 2010. FACULTY: Zvezdana Stojmirovic, MICA, and Helen Armstrong, Miami University.

Fig 43 **TWIN**, 2002
www.letterror.com

This typeface by the Dutch
studio LettError shifts and
mutates according to the daily
weather conditions of the
Twin Cities in Minnesota.

Type Is Modular

Language is a modular system, with grammar providing the rules and alphabets the building blocks. Type designer Erik Spiekermann insists that in order to be legible, typefaces must mostly look alike and be structured out of a system of ascenders, descenders, counters, and other parts of letters, leaving small but important room for stylistic distinction.[1] Illustrated here are two fresh examples of typographic modularity.

1 Gary Hustwit, *Helvetica*, Interview
  with Erik Spiekermann (London:
  Swiss Dots/Veer, 2007).

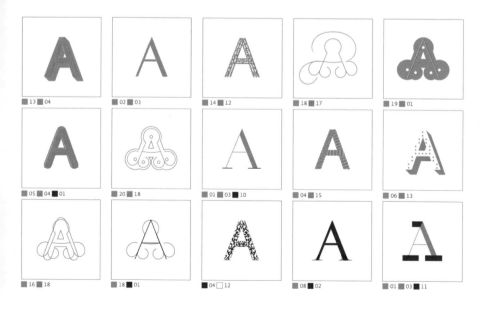

Fig 44 **HISTORY**, 2009
www.typotheque.com/fonts/history

Users can draw from a library
of twenty-one layers to mix and
match the historical traits of
this typeface into deliriously
luscious combinations. Created
by Peter Bil'ak.[2]

2 For an article about the making
  of the font History, see Peter
  Bil'ak, "The history of History,"
  Typotheque website, 2010,
  http://www.typotheque.com/
  articles/the_history_of_
  history (accessed November
  29, 2010).

Type Bits

Experiment with modularity by creating typefaces. In this project, students at Miami University developed bitmap typefaces and learned about the inherent modularity of letterforms.

Like all pixel-based images, bitmap letterforms are described on a map of bits—binary units of information turned either on or off. Vectors, on the other hand, are mathematical functions that render images using lines, not bits. Recently most screen fonts have been vectorized by PostScript and OpenType technology, but the severe constraints of a bitmap-style modular typeface still provide an interesting challenge. The students used various office supply labels to construct letterforms on gridded paper first. They then converted their typeface to vectors to make it functional.

TRY THIS PROJECT

Pick a random text message from your cell phone.

Using office supply labels (squares, circles, or rectangles), construct modular letters that spell out the message.

Convert the letterforms into vector graphics using the Live Trace command in Adobe Illustrator.

Arrange the letters into a full lowercase font.

STUDENT WORK: *(top to bottom) Rachael Fraleigh, Emily Schwegman, Arianne Krekeler, Jennifer Miller. Typography One, Miami University, fall 2010.* FACULTY: *Helen Armstrong.*

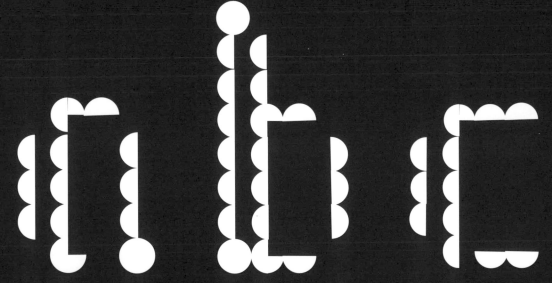

Letter Splice

Explore the modularity of letters by deconstructing classic typefaces and creating your own new forms. In this project, students from Miami University dissected a typeface into parts, which they repurposed as modular units for building a family of icons.[3]

3 This project is based on the interactive website Type is Art (www.typeisart.com), created by Silo Design, where visitors use letter parts to create their own compositions. It is also inspired by the site Bembo's Zoo (www.bemboszoo.com), created by Roberto de Vicq de Cumptich. For a related project, see Ellen Lupton's Helvetica assignment in the book *Design School Confidential: Extraordinary Class Projects from the International Design Schools, Colleges, and Institutes* by Steven Heller and Lita Talarico. Finally, an online tool called Fontstruct (fontstruct.fontshop.com) allows you to build your own modular letterforms with ease.

STUDENT WORK: *(top to bottom) Julia Hustedt, Paige Hake.*
Typography One, Miami University, fall 2010. FACULTY: *Helen Armstrong.*

TRY THIS PROJECT

Pick a classic serif typeface.

Examine the different parts of the characters. Notice that each typeface is broken into the same twenty-one parts, including ascender, descender, crossbar, bowl, counter, and terminal, etc.

Visit typeisart.com to see a description of each part and play around with this site for a bit.

Return to your chosen typeface and dissect it into the twenty-one parts in Illustrator.

Using these parts, create a family of three icons. All three icons should have a common theme (for example: faces, animals, lamps, seasons) and a similar look and feel.

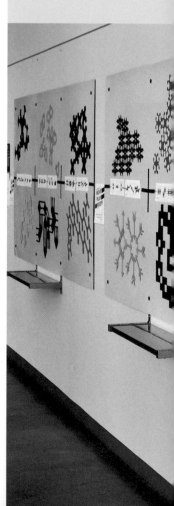

Modules at Play

This three-part project illustrates the modular potential of shapes and teaches aspects of modularity, such as formal repetition, audience interaction, and animation. By drawing vector shapes, setting up an exhibition, and learning Flash animation, MICA students studied these aspects and explored how simple modules can connect to form complex relationships.

STUDENT WORK: *(below) Elizabeth Beasley, Lindi Biery, Daniel Cha, JT Cobell, Greg Cole, Kirsten Gundry, Chris Hurley, Sara Jabbari, Alena Jaffe, Izzy Jarvis, Carla Johnson, Nadia Kabra, Minhee Kim, Harrison Kuykendall, Matt Lewicki, Sarah Straub, Sol Winer, Cameron Wray.*

Graphic Design 1, MICA, fall 2010. FACULTY: *Zvezdana Stojmirovic.*

TRY THIS PROJECT

Draw a shape that can easily be repeated.

Make twelve copies of your shape. Hand-cut them yourself or use a laser cutter.

Display your shapes in a user-friendly way and let an audience arrange and rearrange them.

Document various arrangements throughout the duration of your exhibition.

Use Adobe Flash to create a ten-second animation, showing the different ways in which your module can repeat.

Modularity Tips

Crowdsourcing describes the phenomenon of companies engaging large, loosely defined groups of people in the making of a product. In 2009, for example, the company Netflix awarded one million dollars to a team of scientists for the winning entry in the Netflix Prize, an open call for a better preference algorithm for the video-rental website. Rather than hiring a team of problem solvers, the company chose to have thousands of self-driven programmers compete to improve the existing system. Only the winner was offered a monetary reward. (www.netflixprize.com)

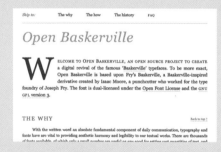

Fig 45 **OPEN BASKERVILLE**, 2009
www.klepas.org/openbaskerville/

Open Baskerville is a crowdsourcing project in typeface design. Started in 2009 and facilitated by Simon Pascal Klein of Mainz, Germany, it is an open call to help draw a revival of the classic typeface. Contributions to the project are made by volunteers via the online platform GitHub's distributed versioning control system and the GNU General Public License, a legal tool protecting co-creation.

4 List taken from Jeff Howe, *Crowdsourcing: Why the Power of the Crowd Is Driving the Future of Business* (New York: Crown Business, 2008), 280–88.

Jeff Howe, whose book *Crowdsourcing* defined the phenomenon, offers ten tips to keep in mind when launching your own crowdsourcing project.[4]

1 **Pick the Right Crowdsourcing Model**
Choose from crowd wisdom, crowd creation, crowd voting, or crowdfunding.

2 **Pick the Right Crowd**
Create a great message and approach the right audiences.

3 **Offer the Right Incentives**
People need to feel rewarded. Attract them and keep them involved.

4 **Keep the Pink Slips in the Drawer**
Crowdsourcing is not a way to circumvent paying your employees.

5 **The Dumbness of the Crowds, or the Benevolent Dictator Principle**
Communities need inspiring leaders.

6 **Keep It Simple and Break It Down**
Make things simple, clear, and modular. People have varying time for involvement.

7 **Remember Sturgeon's Law**
90 percent of everything is crap.

8 **Remember the 10 Percent, the Antidote to Sturgeon's Law**
Don't review all the submissions yourself. Let the crowd help you find the diamonds in the rough.

9 **The Community Is Always Right**
You can try to guide the community, but ultimately you'll wind up following them.

10 **Ask Not What the Crowd Can Do for You, but What You Can Do for the Crowd**
Be transparent and reward your co-creators with respect and reputation.

Modularity is the use of standardized units or sections for easy construction and flexible arrangement. Modularity can apply to the workflow as well as the outcome. The individual pieces, or modules, can be altered or replaced without affecting the remainder of the system.

In their book *Design Rules: The Power of Modularity*, Carliss Young Baldwin and Kim B. Clark define modules as "units in a larger system that are structurally independent of one another, but work together. The system as a whole must therefore provide a framework—an architecture—that allows for both independence of structure and integration of function." Illustrated below are the six different ways described by Baldwin and Clark in which modules can be handled when building a system.[5]

5 Carliss Y. Baldwin and Kim B. Clark, *Design Rules, vol. 1, The Power of Modularity* (Cambridge, Mass.: MIT Press, 2000), 63.

SPLIT

a system into two or more modules

AUGMENT

by adding a new module to a system

INVERT

to create new design rules

SUBSTITUTE

one module design for another

EXCLUDE

a module from the system

PORT

a module to another system

(left) Modules by Alena Jaffe and Nadia Kabra; diagram by Zvezdana Stojmirovic.

Modularity Principles

Aggregation is the amassing of things, people, or data around a common purpose or plan. News aggregation websites pull headlines from disparate sources into a single location for easy viewing. In co-creation projects, self-motivated, diverse participants contribute to aggregate brainpower in creative problem solving. At the close of the twentieth century, committee-led corporate design often yielded bland, lowest-common-denominator solutions, leading designer Tibor Kalman to declare in his 1998 manifesto: "Fuck Committees (I Believe in Lunatics)."[6] Just a decade later, we find with renewed optimism that the Internet has allowed us to collaborate in new, nonhierarchical ways. Teams, self-organized on the web, boast diverse rather than homogeneous talents. The aggregation of parts into a whole that is greater than the individual contributions builds on the collective, expanded capability of the group.

Constraints and parameters are the rules put in place to carry out a modular participatory project. While a constraint is a restriction on what contributors can do (for example, use only two prescribed colors), a parameter reveals the structure of the system in which they are participating (for example, only GIF files will be accepted in a given project). When sourcing out your project to dozens of collaborators, be very clear about the rules of participation, or else your project will descend into muddled confusion. This should come easy to designers, trained from the outset to work within constraints.

Granularity is the extent to which a whole can be broken down into parts. The more components, the finer the grain. Granulation is the process of breaking something down into smaller pieces. In visual culture, a granular project is one composed of many small parts, or a collaborative project in which each participant contributes a small piece.[7]

Reciprocity is the mutual exchange of value. Typically, a payment is made in exchange for a service or a good. Co-creation has disrupted the reign of the monetary reward and has occasioned a new reciprocity, in which contributions are exchanged for nonmonetary rewards, such as reputation, acknowledgment, and a sense of community. Although these rewards are not pecuniary, they are no less valuable. Without them, new economic models that mix free services with paid ones could not exist. The better defined the reciprocity is—how and what you get in return for your participation—the more successful is the project.

6 Michael Bierut, William Drenttel, and Steven Heller, eds. *Looking Closer 4: Critical Writings on Graphic Design* (New York: Allworth Press, 2002), 113.

7 For a discussion on corporate granularity, see Patrick Viguerie, Sven Smit, and Mehrdad Baghai, *The Granularity of Growth: How to Identify the Sources of Growth and Drive Enduring Company Performance* (Hoboken, N.J.: John Wiley & Sons, 2008).

Systematic Thinking In the 1960s Swiss designer Karl Gerstner developed a problem-solving system that strove to make the mechanics of the designer's mind modular. In tackling a new project, he would determine all the requirements and attributes his design needed to have, arrange them in a hand-drawn spreadsheet, and plot out the solution at the intersections. Although this system runs counter to American design pedagogy, which privileges intuitive response over system-atized creativity, it is a useful early example of how the design process can run in a modular way. The attributes arranged in a matrix can be added or taken away, like modules, thereby shaping the design process.[8]

Think of the way you start a new project. Do you string your notes in a narrative way, jot them down as lists, or encapsulate them in single words? Try making a chart like Gerstner's to organize your thoughts, and the features and requirements of the design.

8 Karl Gerstner, *Designing Programmes* (Teufen, Switzerland: Niggli, 1964).

a Basis

1. Components	11. Word	12. Abbreviation	13. Word group	14. Combined	
2. Typeface	21. Sans-serif	22. Roman	23. German	24. Some other	25. Combined
3. Technique	31. Written	32. Drawn	33. Composed	34. Some other	35. Combined

b Colour

1. Shade	11. Light	12. Medium	13. Dark	14. Combined	
2. Value	21. Chromatic	22. Achromatic	23. Mixed	24. Combined	

c Appearance

1. Size	11. Small	12. Medium	13. Large	14. Combined	
2. Proportion	21. Narrow	22. Usual	23. Broad	24. Combined	
3. Boldness	31. Lean	32. Normal	33. Fat	34. Combined	
4. Inclination	41. Upright	42. Oblique	43. Combined		

d Expression

1. Reading direction	11. From left to right	12. From top to bottom	13. From bottom to top	14. Otherwise	15. Combined
2. Spacing	21. Narrow	22. Normal	23. Wide	24. Combined	
3. Form	31. Unmodified	32. Mutilated	33. Projected	34. Something else	35. Combined
4. Design	41. Unmodified	42. Something omitted	43. Something replaced	44. Something added	45. Combined

Fig 46 **KARL GERSTNER, PROCESS CHART.** *Designing Programmes*, 59.

Name

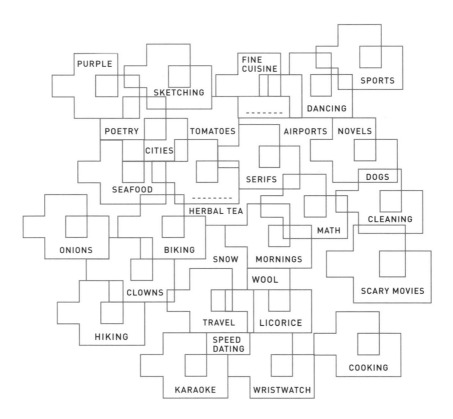

PURPLE

SKETCHING

FINE CUISINE

SPORTS

DANCING

- - - - - - -

POETRY   TOMATOES   AIRPORTS   NOVELS

CITIES

SERIFS   DOGS

SEAFOOD

- - - - - - - -

HERBAL TEA

CLEANING

MATH

ONIONS   BIKING   SNOW   MORNINGS

WOOL

SCARY MOVIES

CLOWNS

TRAVEL   LICORICE

HIKING

SPEED DATING

COOKING

KARAOKE   WRISTWATCH

Who Are You?

Share yourself with the world using this identity signage template. Photocopy the template onto paper of your choice. Fill in the areas that list things that you do not like in one color. Use a second color to fill in areas that indicate things that you like. If you have no feelings toward a topic, leave it blank. If your feelings are complex, mix the colors together. In the dashed lines, fill in your own particular like or dislike. Use your preferences to generate your own identity mark. Hang the sign in your office space or on your dorm room door to reveal your identity to others.

Flexibility

"THE THING WE CREATE SHOULD BE GENEROUS AND CONFIDENT ENOUGH THAT IT ALLOWS YOU TO ADOPT AND ADAPT AND MAYBE EVEN BASTARDIZE IT, BECAUSE THAT TOO IS A FORM OF PARTICIPATION."

IJE NWOKORIE, INTERVIEW BY AUTHORS, 2010

The words *corporate branding* bring to mind solid unwavering marks, accompanied by fat imperious style guides. Participatory culture disassembles such elite singular logos, giving them over to a new breed of designers who revel in the fluctuating, unpredictable form of the flexible mark. Using modules and templates, they build identity systems that empower users, overturning top-down hierarchies long reinforced by modernist design principles.

Modern designers during the first half of the twentieth century pared communication down to its simplest form. After World War Two, the logo business, now the branding business, sprang from newly minted multinational corporations that desired to appear unified, strong, and singular.[1] Designers such as Paul Rand and Lester Beall created detailed identity systems to tame the chaotic diversity of these large entities, including UPS, Westinghouse, ABC, and International Paper Company.

At the same time that the corporate logo soared in the business world, intellectual communities ironically began deconstructing the general concept of singular identity and universal messaging. In the 1960s poststructuralists emphasized the slippery nature of meaning, proclaiming that a single controlled message constructed by an author was impossible. All works, all texts, suggested theorists such as Roland Barthes and Umberto Eco, are "open." Users experience a piece differently with each reading.[2]

In the 1970s and 1980s, postmodern designers, including Katherine McCoy, Lorraine Wild, Dan Friedman, and April Greiman, embraced this concept of multiple meaning by requiring audiences to arduously interpret their

1   For a discussion of the rise of the multinational corporation, see Roland Marchand, *Creating the Corporate Soul: The Rise of Public Relations and Corporate Imagery in American Big Business* (Berkeley: University of California Press, 1998).

2   See Umberto Eco, "The Poetics of the Open Work," in Bishop, *Participation*, 22. And Roland Barthes, "Death of the Author," *Image/Music/Text*, trans. by Stephen Heath (New York: Hill and Wang, 1977), 142–48.

ICON: *(opposite) designed by Daniel Cha*

complex designs.[3] Yet, despite this larger climate of deconstruction and plural-ity, the singular corporate identity, for the most part, remained intact through-out the twentieth century. The Internet of today, bit by bit, is finally chipping away at this solid facade.

Single static marks strain to represent the complex give and take of the contemporary brand. No longer can companies broadcast from high their core messaging, spreading it to passive consumers through an expensive and, therefore, exclusive distribution system. Users now communicate, consume, and create—often simultaneously—as they interact with a brand. Corporations today frantically set up mechanisms for such participation, creating interactive websites for making your own commercials and fanisodes, setting up contests for user-developed products, generating templates for customizing purchases, and publishing blogs filled with brand-related dialogue as well as online corporate magazines seeking user commentary and ratings. At the same time, users engage through their own unofficial channels: blogs devoted to brand gossip, Facebook fanclubs, remixes, mashups, user ratings, and commentary. Sometimes such participation furthers a preset corporate message, but more often users hijack brands, reconstituting them with new meaning.[4]

Designers answer these activated consumers by breaking apart the tradi-tional singular mark. Eddie Opara, founder of Map Office in New York City and more recently a partner at Pentagram, uses the term *transformative* to describe what's currently happening to the nature of brands.[5] In 2004, while working at the studio 2x4, Opara, under creative director Michael Rock, created an early example of flexible branding with his identity system for the Brooklyn Museum. This system consists of one core mark surrounded by a secondary component that morphs into eight basic shapes. This identity, he explains, embodies the idea of brands as "ever-growing into something else," perpetually "unfinished."[6] The designer puts a system into motion and then lets go.

Other examples of this type of flexible identity include Jonathan Barnbrook's identity for Dignity (www.barnbrook.net/dignity.html), an association of

3   For a discussion of postmodern design involving Katherine McCoy and Lorraine Wild at Cranbrook Academy of Art, see Hugh Aldersey-Williams, *Cranbrook Design: The New Discourse* (New York: Rizzoli, 1990).

4   See Bernard Cova, Robert V. Kozinets, and Avi Shankar, *Consumer Tribes* (Oxford: Butterworth-Heinemann, 2007).

5   Eddie Opara, "Insights Design Lecture Series: Eddie Opara" (lecture, Walker Art Center, Minneapolis, Minn., March 9, 2010), http://channel.walkerart.org/play/eddie-opara/ (accessed November 28, 2010).

6   Ibid.

"WE FEEL IT'S A PRIVILEGE TO BE GIVEN A PLATFORM FOR COMMUNICATING, AND WE LIKE TO DISTRIBUTE THAT PRIVILEGE." ADAM MICHAELS, INTERVIEW BY AUTHORS, 2010

UCLA Architecture & Urban Design

UCLA Architecture & Urban Design

Fig 47 **UCLA ARCHITECTURE AND URBAN DESIGN IDENTITY**, 2007
www.pentagram.com

Eddie Opara (while at his former studio, the Map Office) developed this logo for the University of California, Los Angeles Architecture and Urban Design program. After using it for about a year, the architecture school was forced by the greater university to abandon the mark in favor of a more conservative approach. Opara responded by transforming the identity into something even more abstract, which now appears as a motion graphic on the architecture school's home page, www.aud.ucla.edu.

Fig 48 **WALKER EXPANDED**, 2005
www.walkerart.org

The new Walker Art Center's identity is a fontlike system of colors, borders, letters, and vocabularies that allows unlimited iterations.

Fig 57 SPLICE TODAY IDENTITY, 2010
www.posttypography.com
www.splicetoday.com

The Splice Today logo does not only appear in a wide range of preexisting formats, but users can also upload their own versions. This variable format resonates with the young, web-savvy audience of Splice Today, an online start-up magazine. Like the website masthead, which changes each time it is viewed, each stationery or template application employs a different version of the identity.

Fig 58 IDENTITY FOR THE 14TH INTERNATIONAL SHOW OF DRAWINGS/COMICS, 1998
www.mirkoilicdesign.com

The New York–based studio Mirko Ilić Corp. created this identity for the 14th International Show of Drawings/Comics at the Moderna Galerija in Rijeka, Croatia. The identity (shown here in letterhead form) provides empty silver frames (comics frames) that invite users to draw in the individual boxes, thus enacting the serial image making process of creating comics.

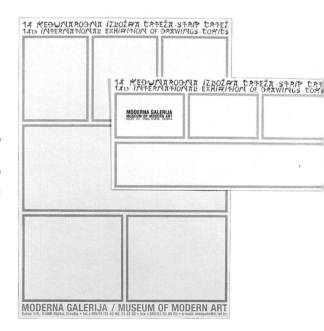

Japanese undertakers, and Andrew Blauvelt's Walker Art Center identity. [Fig 48 and Fig 58] The Dignity logo uses nine circular forms to suggest the cycle of life, while the Walker Art Center identity carries the idea of modularity further by functioning as a typeface. Groups of related words and repeating patterns replace the usual font weights. These lines of words and textures can, like a roll of tape, be applied to virtually anything. Designers can adapt such variable identity systems, adjusting them appropriately for each use.

Often serving as platforms for action, contemporary brands, according to the influential branding firm Wolff Olins, "need to be less controlling, more generous."[7] Both the firm's New York City identity [Fig 55] and their infamous London 2012 Olympic and Paralympic Games mark operate as templates. As opposed to a fixed system of modular parts, any imagery may fill the interior of the letterforms. Such fill-in-the-blank identities encourage, even require, users to supply content, thus encouraging others to leave their own mark.

Some designers have pushed the participatory idea even further into users' hands. While in the preceding examples professional designers ultimately determine the various iterations of their flexible marks, Nolen Strals and Bruce Willen of Post Typography have literally given final form over to the user. Post Typography's branding campaign for Splice Today, an online start-up magazine with a young and web-savvy audience, asks users to draw and submit logos to the growing Splice Today database, which displays the ever-changing mark on the website. [Fig 49] Like the website masthead, each stationery or template application employs a different version of the identity. Every employee's business card reflects a unique logo, which employees may create themselves.

The design studio of Mirko Ilić also opened its identity for the 14th International Show of Drawings/Comics at the Moderna Galerija in Rijeka, Croatia, to the user. [Fig 50] Here the mark functions as a template that remains fixed, while users fill in the content by hand, replicating the storytelling process celebrated in the exhibition. Both the Splice Today and Moderna Galerija logo

7   Wolff Olins, "Brand Next," Wolff Olins website, March–July 2008, http://www.wolffolins.com/brandnext/ (accessed November 11, 2010).

"DON'T FORCE IT. WE'VE ALL SEEN OUR FAIR SHARE OF 'TELL US YOUR SHOELACE STORY'...
CALL TO ACTIONS. PEOPLE ARE PARTICIPATORY BY NATURE, BUT WE HAVE OUR LIMITS."
ERIC HUSBAND, INTERVIEW BY AUTHORS, 2010

systems take full advantage of the concept of identity as template. The designer becomes an enabler, a creator of "vessels or shells" rather than static artifacts.[8] Multiple recent studies argue that when consumers fill in the blanks, they outperform marketers, as consumers have an air of authenticity that is difficult to achieve otherwise.[9]

In some instances, flexible identities rely on technology to imbue systems with varying content. Designer Keetra Dean Dixon and the Amsterdam-based studio Catalogtree have both developed identities that depend upon algorithms to recast logos into unique forms with each iteration. Dixon's identity for the Time and Place Workshop, a small collective heading up the Interaction Lab at Rockwell Group, uses shifting, computationally generated marks to embrace a sense of unpredictability and chance [Fig 75]—appropriate for the collective, which uses interaction and technology to explore time and space. Catalogtree, in collaboration with programmer Lutz Issler, developed a logo for the Rotterdam-based architecture firm Monadnock that manifests differently each time it is saved, exported, or printed. [Fig 53]

By transforming into systems and templates, contemporary brands not only respond to the larger participatory culture, they also reflect the structure of the new corporation. As noted by Wolff Olins, twenty-first-century corporations are more like "constellations" than monolithic entities.[10] Businesses such as Amazon, Etsy, eBay, and Fairtrade comprise vast numbers of retailers and users under their corporate banners. This new business structure, in fact, reflects the larger organization of the Internet itself, an ever-changing elastic network, connecting but not limiting the meaning of its content. Cultural critic Pierre Lévy refers to this structure as "the universal without totality."[11] Starbucks taps into the same idea with their slogan "identity not identical."[12] In contrast to the 1960s, the intellectual community of today lines up with professional practice, as both perceive the same shift toward a network of communities rather than single entities driving culture and commerce.

8 Eddie Opara, "Insights Design Lecture Series: Eddie Opara," http://channel.walkerart.org/play/eddie-opara/ (accessed November 28, 2010).

9 Cova, Kozinets, and Shankar, Consumer Tribes, 21.

10 Wolff Olins, "Brand Next," http://www.wolffolins.com/brandnext/ (accessed November 11, 2010).

11 Pierre Lévy, Cyberculture, trans. Robert Bononno (Minneapolis, Minn.: University of Minnesota Press, 2001), 91–102.

12 Wolff Olins, "Brand Next," http://www.wolffolins.com/brandnext/ (accessed November 11, 2010).

"TECHNOLOGY AND SOCIAL NETWORKING HAVE GIVEN CUSTOMERS NEW POWER TO INTERROGATE THE CHOICES THEY MAKE AROUND PRODUCTS. WE CAN GO ONLINE AND ASK OUR 150 FRIENDS."

IJE NWOKORIE, INTERVIEW BY AUTHORS, 2010

Fig 51 **TYPECON IDENTITY**, 2009
www.underconsideration.com

For "TypeCon," the annual conference organized by the Society of
Typographic Aficionados, Under-
Consideration designers Armin Vit
and Bryony Gomez-Palacio created
a logo that never appeared the
same way twice. Interpreting the
theme of the conference, rhythm,
as "a visual tool that establishes
order yet allows for surprises,"
they designed a mark that does just
that as it reconfigures itself while
maintaining a consistent visual
language.[1]

1   UnderConsideration, "TypeCon
    2009: Rhythm Logo," UnderCon-
    sideration website, http://www.
    underconsideration.com/dod/
    archives/typecon_2009_rhythm_
    logo.php (accessed November
    29, 2010).

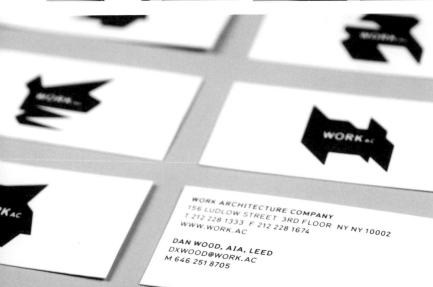

Fig 52 **WORK ARCHITECTURE
COMPANY IDENTITY**, 2007
www. projectprojects.com

Project Projects created this
identity system and variable
logo for Work Architecture
Company (WORKac), combining
a sense of familiarity with an
unexpected changeability. A grid
system underlies the theoretically
limitless set of seemingly random
polygonal shapes.

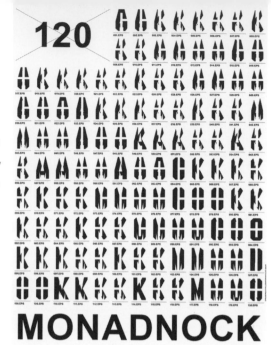

Fig 53 **MONADNOCK IDENTITY**, 2007
www.catalogtree.net

In collaboration with programmer Lutz Issler, Catalogtree created this flexible logo system for Rotterdam-based architects Monadnock. A new iteration of the logo is generated from a PostScript file each time the user saves, exports, or prints it.

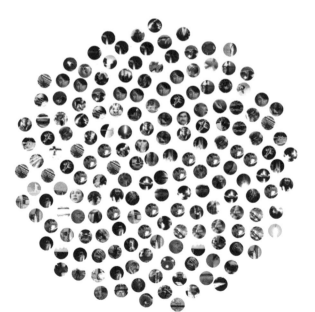

Fig 54 **PHYLOTAXIS**, 2005
www.number27.org
www.phylotaxis.com

Seed magazine commissioned designer Jonathan Harris to develop Phylotaxis, a variation of the original logo for Seed Media, designed by Stefan Sagmeister. Harris transformed the mark, which is based on the Fibonacci sequence, into an interactive system that composes its own new identity every few hours by harvesting fresh Internet data from the fields of science and culture.

Designers need not fear this monumental shift from individual to network, from single artifact to generative system, from corporate mark to flexible identity. For quite some time, they have practiced a complex understanding of templates and systems by working with grids.[13] A grid is, in essence, a system. As Karl Gerstner pointed out in 1963, "[The grid] is a formal programme to accommodate x unknown items."[14] The challenge of a grid is then essentially the same challenge faced by designers of systems today: "the maximum of constraints, with the greatest possible variability."[15] While Gerstner perhaps did not envision that users would be filling his sacred grid with content, designers still tread on familiar terrain. Increasingly unrestricted by production and distribution constraints and spurred on by an eager participatory force, twenty-first-century grids emerge as flexible systems designed not for predetermined content, but for unpredictable users.

Such flexible marks nurture participatory impulses, allowing users to engage head-on with consolidated corporate powers. For years researchers have emphasized consumers' tendency toward self-realization through brands: people figure out who they are through the brands they buy. Recent studies have found that consumption, particularly participatory consumption, is more complex. As activated users consume brands, they form connections with niche communities. This "consumption of cultural resources circulated through markets" facilitates what theorist Bernard Cova terms the "sine qua non of contemporary life": "meaningful social relationships."[16] And that, perhaps, is what participatory culture and design is all about. As designers enable participation, they reinforce fragile niche communities. They empower users to build blocks of communal power that can effectively talk back to brands, engaging them, redirecting them, and, sometimes, hijacking them, for the good of the users' own interests and concerns.

13 For a discussion of grids and graphic design, see Ellen Lupton, *Thinking with Type: A Critical Guide for Designers, Writers, Editors, & Students* (New York: Princeton Architectural Press, 2004), 113–61.

14 Karl Gerstner, *Designing Programmes* (Teufen, Switzerland: Niggli, 1964).

15 Ibid.

16 Cova, Kozinets, and Shankar, *Consumer Tribes*, 5.

"I HAVE LONG THOUGHT SAMENESS IN BRANDING IS OVERRATED. THERE ARE SITUATIONS WHERE A STATIC LOGO MAKES SENSE...BUT THERE ARE MANY OTHER INSTANCES WHERE A VARIED APPROACH TURNS OUT TO BE SUPERIOR." STEFAN SAGMEISTER, INTERVIEW BY AUTHORS, 2010

IJE NWOKORIE

www.wolffolins.com

As a senior strategist at Wolff Olins's London office, Ije Nwokorie uses his knowledge of the big shifts happening in business and culture to build brands. According to Nwokorie, users are no longer satisfied with passively consuming corporate messaging. In a world driven by participatory culture, brands have become platforms for people to do new things.

How is contemporary branding connected to participatory culture?

Branding is driven by participatory culture. Technology and social networking have given customers new power to interrogate the choices they make. We can go online and ask 150 friends about the product through our Facebook site. The customer is not making a decision based on a message that is being spun by an organization. They are making a decision based on real tangible interaction that they, their friends, their family, and millions of people online have had with the product. For a brand to be successful, it needs to focus on the reality of using a product.

Brands can no longer just take a position and defend it with marketing messages, because the customers are going to navigate them. The brand has to define an active and useful role in people's lives. To be able to define that, you have to engage people in defining what it is they want to do. Brands that have risen in the past ten years are brands that have been primarily developed and propagated by their users.

Do you have trouble convincing clients to go in a participatory direction?

There is a general feeling of acceptance that this shift is taking place. But this stuff is happening so quickly that there are still very few successful case studies. The successful examples tend to be new ones, because the bulk of the infrastructure that most companies have are not built for this. They are built for a paradigm of control.

These older systems think: "Invent from within our narrow box and keep everything confidential. When we have tested it in our focus groups, then release it through our product cycles. When we put that out there, it will be another twelve months before we have to invent again."

This doesn't work in a world where customers are demanding newer versions day after day. I think all of our clients get this. What we all struggle with is this: "How do I make that work for a company whose DNA and operating system doesn't lend itself to that?"

Can you talk more about what participatory culture means for your work?

Participatory culture is a defining condition in which we exist. We cannot sit in our office and come up with the thing that millions or even billions of customers are going to love. If we are not plugged into what people are doing right now, we are going to get it wrong. The volume of things that our client organizations have to produce to be relevant today is not doable by them and us. We are going to have to engage huge communities to make that happen. We have to start with participation and collaboration as a fundamental principle of anything we do.

It's important, having said that, to say that our work still requires us to create the seed that inspires people or enables people to participate. They have to come up with the context, the call to action, and the container that will engage people and get them to participate. Increasingly, our job is not to create the thing, but to create whatever allows a broad community of participants to create the thing.

In working with graphic designers, do you think there is a new paradigm in design practice that is influenced by participatory culture?
I am not a graphic designer, so there are probably people better qualified to answer that. But I think that concept is coming through and leading to some wonderful creative expressions. The thing we create is not finished. In other words, the thing we create is generous and confident enough that it allows you to adopt and adapt and maybe even bastardize it, because that too is a form of participation.

When I started in this industry, the corporate identity was a pristine thing. There were all sorts of rules around it. We increasingly see that identities are not inert things; they are much more systems. You want people to appropriate them and make them fit their purposes, because, again, you cannot predict the ways people are going to do this.

Do you think graphic design is destined for obsolescence?
The answer is no. Graphic design, in its broader sense, has never been more important. Design is about making sense of complexity and disorder and making that usable and useful to people.

It isn't about the message and messaging. It isn't about controlling branding elements. It isn't about brand management anymore. It's about giving people things to use. That makes design incredibly important and powerful.

Give some examples of a flexible mark and explain how this flexibility adds value to the brand.
The New York City, AOL, and (RED) marks (which is Bono's charity). [Fig 55, Fig 56, Fig 57] Those marks are signals and I just mean signals, not the entire embodiment of the concept. Their value is what the customer or the user makes of them. They allow people to overpopulate them or procreate them or bastardize them.

(RED) is built to sit alongside other brands. Built into its DNA is the fact that Starbucks, for example, is going to do something with it. It has to lend itself to the things that other brands are doing. New York is such a diverse and wonderful culture, so you fill it with what makes sense to you. A mark becomes a signal to be interpreted: "If I can do that with a mark, then I can make that with a brand itself. I can make New York what I want to make it, and I can use AOL in the way that works for me, and if I'm Starbucks, I'm imagining what I can do with (RED)."

Have you had cases where the interactivity or flexibility of the brand has been problematic?
No, what happens is the brand owners find flexibility hugely liberating. The brand goes from being a straitjacket that says you can't do this and you can't do that, to being an inspiration that says "try this" and "how about that."

What do you feel is important to talk about in terms of branding today?
What does this mean about the practice of developing brands from the client's side? One of the fundamental questions in business today might be, "How do businesses need to change not just culturally, but actually structurally, to be able to respond to this ferocious consumer appetite and the capability that millions of people have to sift through information and make decisions on their own?"

WOLFF OLINS

Fig 55 **NEW YORK CITY BRAND**, 2007
www.wolffolins.com

(opposite) Wolff Olins's identity for New York City represents the kaleidoscopic quality of the city. The mark acts as a window revealing unlimited views of real New York inhabitants and neighborhoods.

Fig 56 **(RED) BRAND**, 2006
www.wolffolins.com

(right top) To achieve its goal of helping eliminate AIDS in Africa, the charity (RED) partners with iconic brands to make unique products. Up to 50 percent of the profits from the sales of these products go toward HIV and AIDS programs. Wolff Olins built the (RED) brand as a flexible visual system designed to embrace partner logos.

Fig 57 **AOL BRAND**, 2009
www.wolffolins.com

(right) As part of AOL's spin-off from its merger with Time Warner, AOL's executive leadership team partnered with Wolff Olins to develop an identity system that telegraphs its shift in focus: a new commitment to becoming a great content brand for all types of consumers. The AOL word mark appears in front of a wide range of images and animations developed in partnership with artists such as Universal Everything, GHAVA, Debut Art, and Dylan Griffin.

ANDREW BLAUVELT

www.walkerart.org

Andrew Blauvelt is design director, curator, and head of the Design Studio at the Walker Art Center in Minneapolis, Minnesota. He coordinates all elements of print design at the Walker Art Center—from exhibitions to museum signage—as well as contributing to programming. In 2005 he developed the Walker Expanded identity, a bellwether for the growing movement toward flexible identities.

You touch on the general design shift toward networked, generative, and contingent solutions in your writing on Relational Design.[1] Why do you think so many flexible branding projects are surfacing right now? What is driving this trend?

The idea of kinetic identities first emerged in the 1980s, and it's a theme that has preoccupied me since that time. The new Walker identity [Walker Expanded] was a response to the concept of a simple application of identity—it's a strip that can be placed on anything, a wall, a letterhead, a brochure, etc.—combined with a complex design system. [Fig 58] The system can be modified by the designers using it. They can not only make choices about patterns but also contribute new patterns to the mix.

A previous identity we did for the web platform mnartists.org was a variable logo whose basic shape changes depending on the rate and category of uploads to the website.

The most recent example of dynamic identities is the one we created for the School of Visual Arts D-Crit program, which uses a traditionally fixed letter mark but an ever-changing picture library of design artifacts. [Fig 60] We think organizations are alive and always changing, not static or monolithic entities. They might need or want an identity that isn't a redo of corporate identity principles.

How does the concept of open source influence your work?

The idea of creating (designing) a system to which people can contribute is an important advancement in a field that is normally tightly held and controlled. But to me "open" doesn't mean free-for-all.

Crowdsourcing logo designs isn't as interesting as crowdsourcing knowledge.

There is a looming fear out there that programming will supplant good old graphic design. What's missing in design education? If you were asked to create a graphic design program for undergraduates, what would be the three most important courses in your curriculum?

Do you mean programming literally? Or do you mean software knowledge? Graphic design students need to be proficient in certain software for layout, imaging, and drawing. Basic motion and web software is important. I think students have to know so much these days—the practice is much more diverse, and all of the work that used to be distributed among many skilled people has gotten integrated into the work of the designer. I'm in favor of an educational experience that is holistic—where students engage in projects fully and comprehensively, no matter what their level is. We used to be able to break it all down and apart and learn it in bits, but there's just not enough time for that now, I think.

Would you say that the campaign for the new Walker marked a shift toward greater audience participation in the museum environment? How has that shift fared since? Could you name another example that speaks to museum-based participation?

Yes, that campaign was a kind of visual precursor to the place that many museums find themselves these days, which is more face to face with their audiences. The larger cultural context has shifted the game as well. People are used to commenting, contributing, and participating in more direct ways. They still like to just watch, listen, reflect, and absorb—and museums are great places for those activities already.

In the summer of 2010 we initiated a new project called Open Field that took place on the museum's front yard (or backyard). It was the first time we really invited the general public to use our space for whatever activities they could imagine. Of course, there were rules, basic ones that you probably find in any city park. We also programmed new activities, then invited the public to participate. There were a wide range of activities, from a communal drawing club that met each week to a series of bull-whipping lessons by a local expert to group yoga for two hundred-plus people. The idea was to create a museum-based platform—another high-tech metaphor—with which people can engage.

With the democratization of design, the fundamental role of the graphic designer is shifting toward mentor/teacher/leader. Do you agree?

Perhaps. I think the role of the designer is still a designer. But instead of designing a fixed, final thing, they are more likely to be designing things people use to create or design other things. Designing design. Designing systems. Designing processes. Designers will be the ones spreading the virtues of what businesspeople call *design thinking* (the design process, the creative process, sustainable innovation, etc.).

Which designers do you think are currently doing the most intriguing work? Who inspires you at the moment?

Oh, too many people, really. I'm not a purist; I have catholic tastes. I like publishing culture and its type geeks and purists, designers who experiment with technologies, a good logotype (traditional or not).

Where do you see the future of typography going? Name two great recent typefaces.

Like other forms of design, typography has been democratized to great effect. It has created a resurgence of interest on the part of designers to create the letterforms they design with as well as enabled much more customization in applications. I've been interested in designers who use fontlike software to create other things.

This was the case with our new Walker identity. It's applied using font software. The multidimensionality of type is also interesting and makes the design more of a conceptual endeavor. I like the idea of a font like History by Peter Bil'ak that uses layering as a strategy, or the dynamic qualities of La Lorraine by Phillipe Apeloig.

What is the most interesting conversation about design that you have had recently?

I'm working on a new exhibition about graphic design, a subject that I have avoided as a curator until now. The field is so diverse and the practice changing so much that it's nearly impossible to summarize it. So I don't think I will be able to.

What three websites do you visit most frequently?

This week it's Design Observer, Huffington Post, and Delta.

Is there anything you would like to add?

Is it okay not to participate?

---

1   Andrew Blauvelt, "Towards Relational Design," *Design Observer*, November 3, 2008, http://observatory.designobserver.com/entry.html?entry=7557 (accessed February 13, 2011).

ANDREW BLAUVELT

Fig 69 **WALKER EXPANDED**, 2005
www.walkerart.org

(opposite) This influential early
flexible identity system transforms
the concept of a set mark into an
overall look and feel constructed
of related words and repeating
patterns. The identity functions as
a typeface and can be applied to
virtually anything.

Fig 70 **WALKER ART CENTER
OPENING CAMPAIGN**, 2005
www.walkerart.org

(right) To coincide with the opening
of the new Walker Art Center, the
institute's design team developed
a promotional campaign called
Where (blank) meets (blank).
The campaign revolved around an
open-ended template in which
users could fill in the blanks with
the range of visual arts, performing arts, and media arts programs
for which the Walker Art Center
is known.

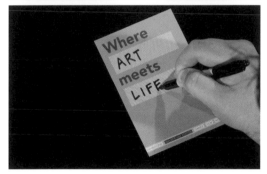

Fig 71 **D-CRIT IDENTITY**, 2008
www.walkerart.org
www.dcrit.sva.edu

The School of Visual Arts MFA
in Design Criticism program,
D-Crit, engaged the Walker Art
Center Design Studio to develop
their new identity. The resulting
mark engages an ever-changing
target of criticism, demonstrating
the wide range of topics D-Crit
students analyze.

BRUCE WILLEN AND NOLEN STRALS

www.posttypography.com

Together Bruce Willen and Nolen Strals form Post Typography, specializing in graphic design, conceptual typography, custom lettering, and illustration with additional forays into art, apparel, music, curatorial work, design theory, and vandalism. Although trained designers, they have what they describe as a "DIY approach to work." In a recent project for Splice Today they embraced flexible identities, opening their mark to user input.

Your identity for Splice Today incorporates lots of other people's work. How did you position yourself in relation to this shift of authorship?
Bruce The idea behind Splice was to build more of a framework than an identity set in stone. [Fig 49] The role of the designer became to create a construct through which the identity can grow. The designer as curator.

There were two concepts that they liked. The current solution was their second choice at first. Then the son of the company owner, a teenager, said, "Dad, this is so much cooler. You have to go for this." The approach made sense for their audience: teens and twenty-somethings. It fits with the online-only nature of the magazine.

Is there any other project in which you used a similar curatorial approach?
B Splice had a lot in common with the Public Print Lab project, although that was more of an art installation. [Fig 61] Both projects developed a framework through which other people could create.

Have any particular difficulties or barriers come up when you have taken on a project like this?
B The challenge is to get users to contribute stuff. In the end it depends more upon the brand, the aura around the company and what they are actually doing. As a graphic designer you can only do so much.

What is inspiring a trend toward participation?
B A lot of it is the hype of the "Internet generation." It's a trend. But, more generally, design tools and the whole design process have become more democratized and widespread. More people know about design and branding and marketing and are willing to see themselves in that position—making a logo, drawing, getting involved. The line between professional and amateur, between business and consumer, and between creator and audience has become blurred.

How do you feel about that blurring of lines?
Nolen It's tough. Part of me wants it to increase. Amateurs could bring design down from the pedestal, the mountaintop. At the same time, there's the issue of the market being flooded with crap. Although amateurs do bring new perspectives, outside points of view. It's a two-edged sword.
B I agree. To a certain extent Nolen and I come from nontraditional design perspectives. We are trained designers but have a DIY approach to work. It fits well with user participation—anyone can become a designer. But at the same time, that shouldn't be a panacea. If everyone is a designer, everything won't necessarily be well designed. "Everyone" can make terrible designs too.

Fig 61 **PUBLIC PRINT LAB**, 2008
www.publicprintlab.com

Post Typography created this
user-generated interactive art
installation in collaboration with
the webzine Beatbots's Justin
Blemly. Users could email or
text images directly to a small
laser printer that Post Typography
had installed in Baltimore's
tiny Minstallation Gallery and
connected to a public email
address. After the close of the
exhibition, an online gallery and
a documentary book displayed
the collected prints.

Flexibility at Work

Community-Activated Design

How do you find the best way to engage the user in the making of your message? Designer Clinton Carlson pursues community-activated design, working together with target audiences to create the messages aimed at them. In 2008 he led a poster campaign on suicide prevention at the University of Nebraska Kearney. Rather than flooding the campus with top-down directives, he placed message-making tools in the hands of the students and watched the campaign design itself. He provided the framework—the templates, stencils, and workshops—while the participants created the end product.

TRY THIS PROJECT

Pick a message and define a local community.

Design a system of posters that remain 80 to 90 percent blank, but have consistent type, color, placement, and orientation.

Develop a library of stencils, which can be both image-based and purely geometric. Posterboard coated on both sides makes a great stencil material.

Determine a simple color palette of three to five colors and prepare latex house paint in these colors with dense, three-to-six-inch-long foam rollers.

Facilitate workshops with community members, and introduce basic design principles, such as repetition, contrast, and cropping, as well as the materials and methods of stenciling.

Ask participants to work quickly and not to worry about being perfect. Each participant should produce ten to fifteen posters in an hour-and-a-half workshop. Encourage experimentation. There are no wrong solutions.

Install the final posters in a place that is accessible to the community.

STUDENT WORK: *(right)*
Participants of the Suicide Prevention Campaign workshops, University of Nebraska Kearney, 2008. FACULTY: *Clinton Carlson, University of Nebraska Kearney.*

STUDENT WORK: *(clockwise from left)*
Lindi Biery, Harrison Kuykendall,
Nadia Kabra

STUDENT WORK: *(opposite)*
Matthew Lewicki
Graphic Design 1, MICA, fall 2010.
FACULTY: *Zvezdana Stojmirovic.*

What's in a Name Tag?

Learn how to design flexible marks for user input by creating a name tag for a fictional speed dating event. Balance the fixed and open-ended elements of your design to create a strong event brand while allowing the user to project his or her personality onto the card. The way you design your template will affect how it will be used.

Sophomore students at MICA were challenged to design name tags to identify and assist participants in the awkward social ritual of speed dating. This project took the online personal profile out of the computer and into physical, social space.

TRY THIS PROJECT

Experiment with grids by drawing three examples. Consider the different ways of organizing information on the page in each of your sketches, and think about the process of filling out forms, both by hand and digitally.

Create three concepts for a speed dating event name tag that is effective in revealing the personalities of the users.

Choose one of your concepts and develop a full layout, considering format and hierarchy. How will the card be worn?

Print ten copies and find ten test users to fill out the cards. Analyze the effectiveness of your layout and finalize the design based on user feedback.

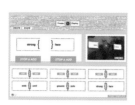

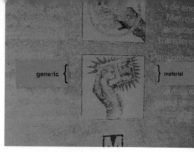

Cameron Zotter's public art sticker tool encourages interaction between the digital and physical environments. Users can make unique stickers online, put them up in physical spaces, and then document and share them with the virtual community.

Create { & } Deploy

Templates and Social Media

Design a template-based online activity. How can templates help facilitate a meaningful user experience? Stemming from grids and forms, the template has historically formed the quiet underside of communication. In this project, it moves front and center.

In a graduate design workshop at MICA, students were asked to identify opportunities for design intervention in everyday life and propose Internet-based solutions. They created prototypes for social media tools that ranged from the poetic to the practical, covering topics such as street art, time management, and travel. The success of each project rested on the clarity and purpose of the students' template designs.

TRY THIS PROJECT

Define *template* and identify different types of templates, such as patterns, tools, procedures, etc.

Brainstorm ideas for the subject matter of your template. Describe the context, user, tool, and template in thirty seconds or less.

Create a set of instructions for how to use the template rather than design the template itself. (In many cases, these steps are intertwined.) Create a sequence, visually and/or verbally, describing how a user would interact with the template.

Prototype the template itself. Use physical and digital means to create sample interface elements and potential user outcomes.

Present your concept in a storyboard-like sequence that illustrates how a product or interface might be used by narrating one or more user scenarios.

An Integrated Calendar iPad Application

Aura Seltzer's iPad application concept merges the two pillars of time management: the daily schedule and the to-do list. Typographic hierarchy, color, and layout are used to make the interface intuitive and easy to use.

STUDENT WORK: *(opposite and this page) Cameron Zotter, Aura Seltzer, Aggie Toppins.*

Graduate Design Studio 1, Visiting Artist Workshop, MICA, *fall 2010.*
FACULTY: *Denise Gonzales Crisp, North Carolina State University, with Brockett Horne and Ellen Lupton,* MICA.

Aggie Toppins proposed this online community for discerning frugal travelers. By assembling albums, users not only organize their own travels but also contribute to the knowledge base that benefits the whole community.

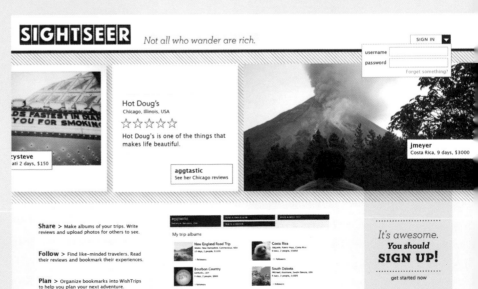

Survey, Surface, Style

Make a piece of participatory fashion. This interdisciplinary assignment draws on audience input as a starting point for product design.

Students at MICA conducted a brief fashion survey among their friends, posing such questions as "What makes a person stylish?" and "Draw your favorite item from your closet." Working in teams, they scanned the handwritten answers and used them to create surface patterns. They went on to print yards of patterned fabric on Spoonflower, an online on-demand fabric printer. Finally, they pooled their skills to design stylish, graphics-driven accessories out of the fabric, including a tube scarf, a kerchief, a bag and notebook set, and a table runner.

WHATS IN YOUR CLOSET?

TRY THIS PROJECT

Write and conduct a short survey.

Let the answers you collect inform your thinking as you decide what product you will design with your fabric. Scan the data, vectorize it, and arrange it into a graphic pattern.

Use an on-demand fabric printing service such as Spoonflower to print your fabric.

Design and make your participatory product.

Document your product. Think of ways to make it accessible to the community that has helped you create it.

STUDENT WORK: *(opposite)* TUBE SCARF: *Megan Barber, Lindi Biery, Sohyoung Kwon, Kate Weintraub.* TOTE AND NOTEBOOK: *Ashley Campbell, Tina Engelmann, Charde Fuller, Staci Maloney.* TABLE RUNNER: *Julian Haddad, Jamie Kimak, Leslie Ortiz, Colleen Roxas.*

SILK SCARF: *(right) Kyle England, Michele Feldman, Elizabeth Orr, Djamika Smith.*

Fashion Graphics, MICA, *fall 2010.* FACULTY: *Zvezdana Stojmirovic.*

Fig 62 **SPLICE TODAY**, 2010.
www.w.posttypography.com

The logo for the online magazine Splice Today changes frequently as readers submit background shapes for inclusion. This open-ended approach is an example of designers sharing control with users.

Fig 63 **TIME AND SPACE WORKSHOP**, 2008
www.fromkeetra.com

In Keetra Dean Dixon's generative flexible design for the Time and Place Workshop, random, computer-generated form, balanced with controlled typography, suggests infinite variations.

Flexibility Principles

Flexibility is the ability of a system to accommodate variations without compromising integrity. Think of flexibility as an approach to culture at large as well as a formal design quality. To be flexible is to be adaptable, responsive to change. Today's shifting networked culture demands of us a mental flexibility, as change and innovation prompt us to think less in terms of finished products and more in terms of open-ended systems.

A flexible brand identity accommodates change, be it purely formal, user-generated, or computational. Traditionally, the graphic mark, fortified by a rigid system of elements and guidelines, defines and distinguishes a product in the eyes of the public. Add to this flexibility, and you get a new kind of branding that embraces flux, shifts, and permutations. It demands of us as designers a certain ceding of control to the end user or the machine. Illustrated here are two kinds of flexible identities: **open-ended** and **generative.**

**Stefan Sagmeister's Tips
for Designing a Flexible Identity**

1. Pick the right project. Make sure there is clear purpose to the flexibility.
2. Pick a direction: finite, open-ended, or generative.
3. Think of it partly as educating the client and the users.
4. Embrace user contributions; it will be an ongoing/long-term relationship.
5. Consider who will be implementing it. Make sure they're on board and competent.[1]

1   Stefan Sagmeister, interview by the authors, July 15, 2010.

"ELASTICITY IS THE ABILITY TO NEGOTIATE CHANGE AND INNOVATION WITHOUT LETTING THEM INTERFERE EXCESSIVELY WITH ONE'S OWN RHYTHMS AND GOALS." PAOLA ANTONELLI, *DESIGN AND THE ELASTIC MIND*, 2008

Templates and Forms

Templates are vehicles for information flow between designer and user. This flow can happen both ways.

From User to Designer: User participation is facilitated by a clear, well-organized system. Templates are blank formats made to be filled in by participants. Think of the interface of your blog, your photo sharing site, or your social network page. Each contains discrete fields for adding and tagging text and images. As the workhorses of participation, templates have emerged from obscurity. Their functionality, look, and feel have become central to the work of designers.

From Designer to User: Conversely, templates can also be ways for a designer to share information with an audience, as Paula Scher did in her 2007 templates for Hewlett-Packard. [Fig 64]

BOLD
MODERN
ELEGANT
friendly
EDGY

Ellen Lupton's Tips for Designing Templates

Keep these questions in mind when designing a template: How do templates work? What are their social and aesthetic features? What role does "user friendliness" play? How is misuse accommodated? What is the visual and interactive interplay between the tool and the outcome? What factors might motivate the targeted user? Is the tool a means to an end? How much user agency does the system allow or inspire? How much know-how is required of the user?[2]

2   Ellen Lupton, email to the
    authors, December 1, 2010.

Fig 64 **THEMES FOR HEWLETT-PACKARD TEMPLATES**, 2007
www.pentagram.com/en/
new/2007/08/paula-scher-designs-free-templ.php

Paula Scher's templates for Hewlett-Packard are designed to help cash-strapped businesses improve their visual output by choosing from several themed stationery templates and filling in their own content. In this way, the designer shares value with the user.

COPY LAND ABRIC
COMBINE

Instructions

1 Make up a rule for cutting into these letters. Alter only the white areas. Here, in no particular order, are some examples of rules:

   a) Cut a crosswise incision into every other diagonal section.

   b) Carve away the opposing corners or curves of each letterform by cutting out triangles.

   c) Using your knife add dimension to the letterforms by freeing segments of the letters and pulling them away from the page. The free segments can be curled, crinkled, etc.

2 Follow your established rule to make cuts or tears into the letterforms.

3 Flip over your sheet to see your own original letterforms appear!

The Human Machine

Turn yourself and your friends into human machines. First read the instructions above and develop a set of rules for the project. Then photocopy this exercise, pass it to ten participants, and get started. Each participant should use your algorithmic process to customize their type. Compare results only when finished. Notice how differently each human interpreted the same set of rules.

Technology

"THE BENEFIT OF WORKING WITH ACTUAL PROCESSES IS THAT THEY ARE PARAMETRIC AND CAN BE RECOMBINED, EXTENDED, AND SHAPED IN INFINITE WAYS. THIS RECOMBINATION OFTEN PRODUCES EXCITING, UNEXPECTED RESULTS, LEADING ONE ON A MEANDERING PATH OF SERENDIPITY." KARSTEN SCHMIDT, INTERVIEW BY AUTHORS, 2010

An understanding of code can push designers toward more process-driven approaches fed by user content and serendipity. For the last one hundred years, designers have worked to transform complexity and chaos into clarity and simplicity. Generative design turns this modernist ethos upside-down. Through process-driven approaches designers mimic the natural world by building complex systems and messaging out of simple steps.[1]

1   See Luna Maurer, interview by the authors, October 7, 2010.

Generative designers produce work with algorithms at the core. They break their design process into steps to be encoded and then followed repeatedly. Each iteration possesses the possibility of a unique expression. Suddenly a thousand unique versions are no more expensive to design and produce than a thousand copies of a single solution. Once the algorithms have been established, iterations of generative projects, in essence, design themselves. In contrast to more traditional form making, designers focus on setting up parameters rather than creating a finished product.

Generative designs are not by necessity participatory projects, as algorithmic systems can be fully automated and self-contained, with no outside data involved. However, many generative designers do invite user contributions or mine outside data sources. The unpredictability of such contributions adds a random element, spicing up the automated nature of the system. For example, artist Julius Popp's machine Bit.Fall (www.sphericalrobots.com) pulls words from the Internet, displaying each momentarily via falling water. A preset group of words appearing in a looped sequence would not have the same effect. It is the unpredictable nature of the content, and its constant reference to the larger culture, that draws the user into the experience.

Along the same lines, the Dutch interactive design studio LUST created A Poster Wall for the 21st Century for the Graphic Design Museum in Breda, the Netherlands. [Fig 65] This automated display generates six hundred unique posters daily by gathering random Internet content. Another LUST project, Scraper, uses Google news RSS feeds to generate a typeface based on user input. [Fig 72] At no given moment can the user, or the designers themselves, predict the upcoming visual form and content of these projects. After decades of exacting, carefully controlled layouts empowered by Adobe software, this serendipitous quality adds a spirited unknown to the work. Technology gave us control in the 1990s; now it opens our work to chance.

The influx of outside content makes such process-oriented projects participatory, whether users are aware of their contributions or not. In his project We Feel Fine, designer Jonathan Harris, in collaboration with Sep Kamvar, collects online personal data surrounding human emotion. [Fig 68] The designer becomes a storyteller, plucking user content from the Internet and then framing and sharing it with others. Every few minutes, this system seeks online occurrences of "I feel" and "I am feeling." The collected phrases, along with basic demographic information, are saved to an ever-growing global archive of human emotions. Since 2005 Harris's system has collected thirteen million feelings. By creating alternative views of the targeted data, We Feel Fine directs users to construct narratives about the individuals behind the feelings. Data mining projects such as this one speak to shifting concepts of privacy and copyright. Once technology translates emotion into data, it is available for the taking.

Harris also develops projects that more actively seek user contributions. For the Yahoo! Time Capsule, Harris requested submissions for a digital time capsule, whose contents were then projected onto the ancient canyon walls of the Jemez Pueblo, a sacred site in New Mexico, for three consecutive nights in 2006. [Fig 66] In the twentieth century, designers typically developed projects that communicated client messaging. Here, in sharp contrast, user content, harvested or contributed, becomes the key message to be disseminated.

"PROGRAM OR BE PROGRAMMED."

DOUGLAS RUSHKOFF, *PROGRAM OR BE PROGRAMMED*, 2010

Fig 65 **A POSTER WALL FOR THE 21ST CENTURY**, 2008
www.lust.nl

The graphic and interactive design studio LUST, based in the Hague, designed this poster wall to commemorate the opening of the new Graphic Design Museum in Breda, the Netherlands. The poster wall exists both online and as an installation in the museum. Each day, the museum installation automatically harvests content from the Internet to generate six hundred unique posters. The online version produces a new poster every five minutes.

Fig 66 **TIME CAPSULE**, 2006
www.timecapsule.yahoo.com

Commissioned by Yahoo!, Jonathan Harris developed the Time Capsule to reflect the human world in 2006. For this project, he asked people to respond to specific questions through text, pictures, videos, sounds, or drawings. Each of the questions stemmed from ten universal themes (love, sorrow, anger, faith, beauty, fun, past, hope, now, and you).This user-generated content was then projected onto the canyon wall of the Jemez Pueblo for three consecutive nights.

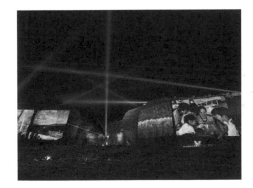

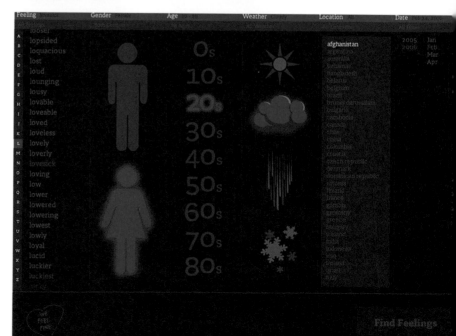

Fig 67 **DAYTUM**, 2008
www.daytum.com
www.feltron.com

The free online statistical resource Daytum, designed by Nicholas Felton, in collaboration with Ryan Case, provides users with a platform for recording and visualizing microdata. Daytum grew from Felton's habit of producing yearly statistical records of his life called "Annual Reports," which he has created since 2005.

Fig 68 **WE FEEL FINE**, 2006
www.number27.org
www.wefeelfine.org

Jonathan Harris teamed up with Sep Kamvar to develop the interactive piece We Feel Fine, which continually harvests sentences containing the phrase "I feel" or "I am feeling" from the Internet's newly posted blog entries. The collected phrases are then saved in a database and displayed in an interactive Java applet. Users can filter the information by demographics to see the emotions in various contexts. We Feel Fine collects around fifteen thousand new feelings per day and has archived over thirteen million feelings since 2005.

Designer Nicholas Felton, like Harris, provides frameworks that transform user content. In 2008 Felton, in collaboration with Ryan Case, created a free online statistical resource called Daytum, providing users with a platform for recording and visualizing microdata—cups of coffee consumed in a day, distance walked, aspirins taken. [Fig 67] The algorithmic structure of the site turns personal data into clear visuals, emphasizing the personal habits that structure our lives, without flattening them into sameness.

An algorithm, by its very nature, is based on input of certain data, which is then output—transformed into something else.[2] This translational motion provides the crux of generative participatory design projects. Designers develop algorithmic structures, users feed those structures with content, and out of the process emerges something entirely new and, sometimes, unforeseen.

Designer Karsten Schmidt (in the online community also known as Toxi) effectuates this transformative motion throughout his work. For the generative identity he developed for the Victoria and Albert Museum's (V&A's) 2009 show Decode: Digital Design Sensations, Schmidt developed an initial code-based logo and then urged users to remix and recode his open source design using a graphic user interface freely available online. [Fig 83] The alternative user versions were displayed in the exhibition's digital gallery and on London Underground digital screens to promote the exhibition.

Schmidt's project shows that encoding their work allows designers to not only create frameworks that respond to user content, but also open the frameworks themselves to manipulation. The designer sets a process into motion and then steps back and watches his or her work play out. Not only was the logo's underlying code open source, but Schmidt also revealed his personal method of developing the initial code online.

The Decode identity exhibits a sense of reciprocity that is central to Schmidt's work. His generous attitude flies in the face of twentieth-century protective stances toward design files and knowledge. Schmidt strives to turn each of his client-funded projects into open source tools and systems that

2   For further discussion about the concept of an algorithm, see Andrew Goffey, "Algorithm," in *Software Studies: A Lexicon*, Leonardo Books, ed. Matthew Fuller (Cambridge, Mass.: MIT Press, 2008), 15–20.

"CREATING COMPUTER SOFTWARE IS THE CLOSEST WE CAN GET TO PURE MENTAL CREATION— SECOND PERHAPS ONLY TO CREATIVE WRITING." AARON KOBLIN, INTERVIEW BY AUTHORS, 2010

others can build upon. Designers, according to Schmidt, should use their projects to continually strengthen the shared knowledge base of the community, to create "permanent value."[3] They should develop technological building blocks that push the whole discipline forward. As he writes, "Technology is not something we just buy in a shop and play around with but something we shape."[4]

Schmidt's ongoing project toxiclibs.org, a collection of open source code building blocks, makes this ethos even more apparent. By creating tools for others to use, he encourages designers to take hold of technology, urging them to consider Douglas Rushkoff's mantra: "Program or be programmed."[5]

Designers such as Harris, Felton, and Schmidt look to code as a way of empowering their work in a complex, rapidly shifting society. Not only do they resist being overwhelmed by the bevy of technology currently available, they pass on their knowledge by creating freely accessible online tools, programs, and lectures. Their work dematerializes the design solution by transforming it into a shareable process. Such a shift not only democratizes design, but also frees projects from hard limitations of medium. The dematerialized coded process can dip in and out of material form, becoming alternatively print products, motion graphics, or sculptural elements. The production headaches of converting designs into multiple media fade as programming literacy empowers designers to move closer to the machine. Code becomes a tool to be wielded at will rather than the mysterious, and limiting, backend of design software.

The Body

While the digital realm drives this shift from finished product to process, the fundamental concept of developing a generative system and then opening it to outside input manifests both inside and outside of the Internet. Some generative designers invite an influx of human labor as the random element of their systems. The human hand disrupts the control of algorithms, adding life to the work. As noted by Dutch-German designer Luna Maurer, "Randomness does

3   Karsten Schmidt, "Real Fake" (lecture, "Real Fake" symposium, University for Art and Industrial Design, Linz, Austria, May 28, 2010).

4   Ibid.

5   Douglas Rushkoff, *Program or Be Programmed: Ten Commands for a Digital Age* (New York: OR Books, 2010).

"THE BEAUTY OF OPEN SOURCE IS YOU DO NOT NECESSARILY NEED TO UNDERSTAND ALL THE EQUATIONS AND ALL THE BEHAVIOR IN UTMOST DETAIL. YOU ONLY NEED TO USE THEM."
KARSTEN SCHMIDT, "REAL FAKE" SYMPOSIUM, 2010

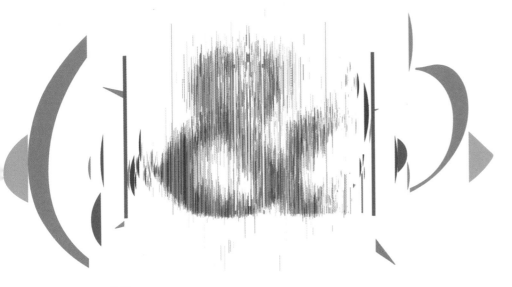

Fig 69 **SLITSCAN TYPE GENERATOR**, 2005
www.c71123.com

Developed by designer J. K. Keller, this Illustrator script types a letter using every font installed on a computer. It then aligns all the letters, cuts slices out of each letter, and recombines the slices into new letterforms.

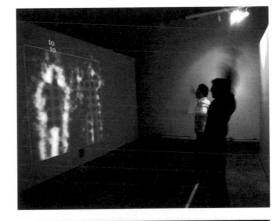

Fig 70 **AFTERWORDS**, 2005
www.bwco.info

Created by Belle & Wissell for the Help Wanted: Collaborations in Art exhibition at the Center on Contemporary Art, Seattle, this interactive art installation reflects the physical movements of participants. Text labels follow them on the screen, combining to create a deeper level of storytelling and interactivity as multiple users enter the space. Interactive artist Randy Moss led the development of the concept and the software that powers this piece.

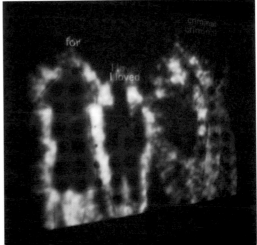

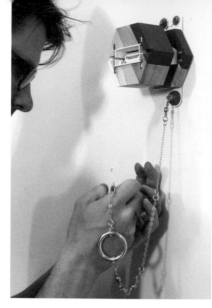

Fig 71 **YOU COULD TELL THEM**, 2008
www.fromkeetra.com

In her gallery piece You Could Tell Them, designer Keetra Dean Dixon encourages users to participate in the exhibition by communicating with one another. Using the provided wall-mounted stamp, visitors leave imprints on their palms. Following the exhibition instructions, they then contribute to the message content by handwriting on the imprint and revealing the message to someone else.

Fig 72 **SCRAPER**, 2007
www.lust.nl

Scraper, an application developed by LUST, uses Google news RSS feeds to generate a typeface based on user input. To initiate the application, users type a phrase or series of characters. The requested characters then materialize as Scraper generates five text weights—light, regular, medium, bold, and black—from either current news feeds or an archive of previous results for that specific user query.

6 Luna Maurer and Roel
Wouters, "Decoding and
Graphic Design Seminar"
(lecture, Graphic Design
Festival Breda, Breda, the
Netherlands, May 25, 2010).

not have to be artificially infused into a system. Human input can take care of that."[6] User participation in these cases occurs through physical motion.

In 2009 Maurer, in collaboration with Roel Wouters, created a graduation catalog for Media Design and Communication at the Piet Zwart Institute Willem de Kooning Academy at Rotterdam University. Through this project, titled *Huh? Oops…Fuck! Oh…Oh, no! Wait…Again…*, Maurer and Wouters transformed a physical artifact into an open-ended design. [Fig 82] Although the catalog was mass-produced using standard digital technology, students, staffers, and designers hand-numbered every one of the book's forty-eight thousand pages. The page numbers, written in charcoal, break down as the catalog is read, contaminating the pages with streaks and smears, both changing the design and emphasizing the handcrafted element of the piece. Each time users handle its pages, they transform the catalog. The algorithmic process, in this instance, is the digital printing process itself—a mechanized series of steps that are followed exactly to create identical copies. The smearing of the charcoal, the result of user motions, disrupts the repetitive nature of this process by transforming what was, in the last century, a finished artifact, into an open-ended design.

Designer Keetra Dean Dixon produces similar process-driven work articulated through physical artifacts infused by human touch. In her gallery piece *You Could Tell Them*, Dixon uses an analog stamp to bring messaging to an individual level. [Fig 71] A wall-mounted stamp leaves an imprint on the palm of gallery guests, who are then invited to complete the imprint by handwriting on their own palm and showing their message to someone else. The communication process becomes a system of rules to be followed by the user, reinterpreted in turn by each physical interaction and ensuing personal message.

As Maurer and Wouters's catalog and Dixon's gallery piece show, generative work is not limited to the digital domain, but there is room for automation and

"I WANT TO COMBINE THE SYSTEM AND THE LOGIC WITH THINGS OUTSIDE THE COMPUTER, ILLOGICAL THINGS. THERE IS A TENSION THERE. I LIKE TO COMBINE TECHNOLOGY AND THE PHYSICALITY OF THE DIRTY WORLD." LUNA MAURER, INTERVIEW BY AUTHORS, 2010

craft, data input and human labor. The crucial element lies not in the medium but in the give and take that occurs between user input and system within each iteration of the process.

This branch of generative design also speaks to the flourishing larger craft movement.[7] Computers, as noted by Puckey, "demand a precise voice."[8] Code must be clear, scrubbed of human ambiguity. Infusing the human touch into algorithmic work muddies its precision. This individual, bodily quality pulls the audience in, warming the inhuman clarity of code. Even though most users experience projects such as Maurer's, Wouters's, and Dixon's as digital images posted online rather than in the physical space they originally inhabit, the sensuality of the work radiates nonetheless. This confluence combats the deficiencies of both craft and code, allowing generative work to evolve in both the physical and digital world.

The New Literacy

Programming is the designer's new literacy. In the twenty-first century, design authorship means access to the code. Open source tools welcome use without requiring full comprehension of the underlying programming structure. This efficiency encourages designers to experiment in ways previously prohibited by the need for in-depth technical mastery.[9] Code easily intimidates, but, by partnering with hardcore programmers as needed, and by both using and constructing open source tools, designers can avoid losing agency to technology.

The algorithmic nature of code provides a backbone for many participatory projects. Process moves front and center in this work as clear steps are encoded and shared, inviting participation by designer and user alike. In a newly activated participatory culture, generative designs cannot be underestimated.

While some designers worry that in an algorithmic world their work will be replaced by technology and automation, the projects highlighted in this section show that designers add an important level of narrative, a context, to a larger generative project. They frame user input in an accessible way, revealing meaning in the data, and structure random human input into provocative output.

Designers also bridge the sterility of code by providing users aesthetic joy. The beauty of images produced by the likes of Harris, Felton, Schmidt, Maurer, and Dixon does not typically flow from the fingers of computer scientists and mathematicians. Design reaches out to other disciplines, and they are reaching out to us. Never has design been so needed.

7   For further reading about the current craft movement, see Faythe Levine and Cortney Heimerl, *Handmade Nation: The Rise of DIY, Art, Craft, and Design* (New York: Princeton Architectural Press, 2008).

8   Jonathan Puckey, interview by the authors, October 14, 2010.

9   Karsten Schmidt, interview by the authors, November 7, 2010.

Fig 73 **OUTRACE**, 2010
www.outrace.org
www.kramweisshaar.com

Clemens Weisshaar and
Reed Kram of the Munich-
and Stockholm-based office
Kram/Weisshaar designed this
installation on Trafalgar Square
during the 2010 London Design
Festival. Through a simple online
interface users could control
eight industrial robots on loan
from Audi's production line to
"write" a personal message in
light traces. The messages were
then sent back to participants
as videos to be shared.

Fig 74 **HEKTOR**, 2002
www.hektor.ch
www.scriptographer.org

Jürg Lehni created Hektor, a
portable spray-paint output
device for laptop computers, in
collaboration with engineer Uli
Franke. Lehni based Hektor's
software on Scriptographer,
a scripting plug-in for Adobe
Illustrator also developed by
Lehni. Hektor, like Scriptographer
itself, demonstrates Lehni's philosophy that tools guide designs
and belong in the hands of the
user, but not as the end product
of closed, inaccessible systems.
In 2008 Hektor inspired Viktor,
a similar drawing machine, but
using four motors instead of two.
Viktor can handle bigger surfaces
and includes tools that require
that a certain type of pressure
is put on the surface it draws on,
such as chalk.

KEETRA DEAN DIXON

www.fromkeetra.com

Keetra Dean Dixon thinks beyond medium as she develops conceptual frameworks for user-driven work. In her design process, she looks first to the concept, then to the experience that can best drive it, and, finally, to the technology needed to make it happen. The resulting projects feel magical, as seamless technology produces unexpectedly playful results. Dixon recently gave up her New York–based studio to accept a teaching position at MICA*.*

Your work incorporates both technology and craft, impersonal code merging and colliding with human touch. Can you speak to the tension between technology and the human body?

I love the phrasing of this question because it reflects the general viewpoint of coding. I understood coding as impersonal myself, until I began partnering with coders. Then I started to understand how technology is an extension of the human effort to make things happen. All tools are technology. Code is a language. It becomes an extension of whoever is offering it, so everybody's code is a unique voice.

I think about graphic design from an experiential point. It's outside restrictions of the medium. A lot of my work involves magic and play and surprise. That means orchestrating something out of the ordinary, so you have to go to unexpected means to make it happen. If technology functions seamlessly, it feels magical. I use technology to make the magic happen. Old school interaction/technology often integrates with the new school version of it.

People often see code as a nonhuman entity, but it's really so marked by its maker.

It's a language, and you are speaking a language to solve a problem. We are talking to our computer or our hardware or etc., etc.

Can you give some examples of projects that you felt had this sort of magic?

A project called Wonder Kept comes to mind. [Fig 76] I tried to capture moments of wonder or suspended moments of vulnerability. There was a bubble bottle sitting on a table. The table was enclosed behind a curtain, creating a photo boothish space with a mirrored wall. Participants were invited to blow bubbles and look at themselves in the mirror. Every time you blew, a photo was snapped behind the mirror, capturing the moment of a person seeing their bubble emerge. That was seamless and magical. Outside of this sheltered booth, images of this action were being projected, so people knew that there was going to be some sort of documentation, but there was no actual interaction. There were no wires and you didn't hear a click. All of those cues were hidden.

You move fluently from low-tech to high-tech. How do you teach a young designer an appreciation for unpredictability within graphic design?

I don't know if you can teach somebody to be comfortable with unpredictability. It's a personality type. There is a specific way that I'm comfortable with it. Often I set up a platform and ask a question in one way or another and then invite people to come in. It's a conversation, a call and response. I get to do a certain amount of things in the process before that unpredictability factor comes in.

It's a prepared unpredictability, right?

There is still a lot of control on my part. It's vital to the evolution and adaptation of graphic design to start out by thinking of things not married to the medium. If we could do anything, what would it be about? What is the overriding concept? Establish the experience that drives that and then apply it within mediums.

What are the essential key ingredients to a successful participatory project?

You must acknowledge the potential audience. There has to be enough room for input into the system, enough flexibility. You need room for participation.

Relinquishing control, openness, and an incredible amount of patience are all key. You also need a lot of testing to be sure the visual system actually functions and results in something, because there has to be a continued call and response. A lot of these things end up being conversations. I make a platform or I ask a question, and then there is a response from the audience. To keep people engaged, it must go back and forth. Whatever platform I put out there needs to keep their interest peaked.

There is a looming fear among designers of not being able to keep up with technology. People are afraid they are becoming obsolete. Do you think graphic design is moving toward obsolescence?

No. Maybe it's because I am concerned about my own survival. I think absolutely technology is overwhelming. I am definitely not a technologist proper. I'm not an expert in any technology. I am a jack of all trades and the master of one. The master of one would probably be graphic design, but some days I question that.

The key is to keep things in perspective. This is difficult, especially when we are being inundated with requests to perform, perform, perform, know it all, answer all the questions all the time. Try to look at the problem more abstractly and understand the general principles being exercised. Take a step back before examining the medium and think about the experience. Consider what the database structure might be, what the variables are within it, and how you might work within those variances.

An individual person authors code, so if you are partnering with someone who is writing code, then you are partnering with a unique author with a unique opinion. Understand there are no steadfast rules. You need to know when to ask for help, be naïve, and when to push. It's all about being willing to learn, being patient, and getting the overall understanding of what things are progressing towards.

I feel that the next big wave is going to be networked objects. There have been baby steps all over the place in that direction. We have a bazillion baby screens linked together all of a sudden. Now these screens are becoming embedded in other forms that aren't our devices or tools for management or our computers. Instead, they are being embedded in our chair or table, so technology will be more ubiquitous.

I don't know how to design for those things. Nobody knows how to yet, which is great. We get to invent our own future at this point. What I do understand is the tendency towards networked objects. I pay attention when new things come out.

Do you think it's coming full circle from this century's departure into technology, the screen, the digital, back to the body?

I have a bit of a theory about that. When I was going to school as an undergrad and all of those guys were taking interactive design, a lot of them partnered old technology with new technology. One guy did a rope and a pulley that was simply hooked up to a computer. It measured revolutions of the pulley and then linked that to a digital display of what was being hauled up.

Now we have digital natives that are doing programming—iPad app development, computation, and hardware stuff. They are replaying the marrying between old tech and new tech, but they have the capability of networking objects. These up-and-coming kids are learning without the definition of interaction as a website. For them, it's more about embedding Arduino in this and that.

They stem from a technological start, whereas we, and those before us, stemmed from something else, the so-called physical or tactile. Because those kinds of technologies are more available and are being introduced as open platforms, the approach of mixing technology with the physical world is new again. A majority of the resulting projects are going to be interaction design. There is no question that it's participatory.

You mention we are entering another period where things are open. Would you speak to the ways that the context of open source is enabling that kind of experimentation?

There is often a misunderstanding about what open source is. It's not a relinquishing of copyright or intellectual property. It's entered into voluntarily, and you can specify whether you want to be credited and how you want to be credited. Essentially, it's sharing. I think it's born out of guys doing interaction when it was just in its infancy. The community, the people who were doing the same kind of work, fit into the palm of their hands.

There wasn't anyone who was a real expert, so they taught one another. That was how they learned: they shared. The thing became a collaborative process. It's the same now.

There are only a handful of people doing these things. The people doing both the hardware development and software development know almost everybody involved in the field. They are always online and trying to figure out these things together. It's not a choice really.

Who makes the profit when people solve problems in small, networked teams?

That's starting to come into play now. These exact things are being utilized and somebody's name has to be credited on the thing, and there is major funding involved, etc. The legality is going to get messy pretty quickly. So far in my experience in the culture, everybody has gotten paid and has gotten their fair share.

What advice do you have for a young designer today?

Try to keep a perspective on the general trajectory of media. Think of things experientially and a little bit "blue sky" before restricting yourself. Be as informed as possible. Be okay with not knowing and ask questions all the time.

The people of yesteryear expected graphic design expertise and that was that. The knowledge was fixed. We are now in an era of questioning.

Designers during the 1950s and 1960s were able to be self-reliant in a way that technology doesn't allow now. You can't be a master of one thing. You have to reach out to people because it's impossible to keep up with one thing yourself by mastering all of the technology required to do it.

Relinquish control in collaborative making for participatory culture. It's how we have to exist now. The first step is being okay with not knowing how it's going to happen, and then proceeding and making it happen.

KEETRA DEAN DIXON

Fig 75 **TIME AND PLACE WORKSHOP IDENTITY**, 2007
www.fromkeetra.com

In this identity for the art/design collaborative group Time and Place Workshop, Dixon uses a generative system of marks that tap into the group's ethos of unpredictability and chance.

KEETRA DEAN DIXON

Fig 76 **WONDER KEPT**, 2007
www.fromkeetra.com

(opposite) In Wonder Kept, Dixon
documents the seconds of antici-
pation, vulnerability, and splendor
that lie in the act of blowing a soap
bubble. For this installation, Dixon
created a photo booth–like space,
in which participants trigger a
hidden camera each time they lift
a bubble wand and blow a bubble.
The camera captures the moment
in which people see their bubble
emerge. Willing Wonder is an
ongoing companion collection of
the bubble-blowing portraits.

Fig 77 **SENSITIVE**, 2010
www.fromkeetra.com

(below) Dixon's SENSitive study
partners the unpredictability of
material structure with rudimen-
tary tools. Clay is fed into a
small-scale extruder fitted with a
custom-type template to produce
three-dimensional clay letters.
The piece is a study for a future,
much larger, publicly located
installation that will invite users
to feed bricks into a machine,
squirting out foot-tall letters.

Fig 78 **PLUG-IN-PLAY**, 2010
www.fromkeetra.com

(above) Plug-in-Play, developed
by Dixon together with the
Interaction Lab at Rockwell
Group, is a visual system for a
projected virtual city. The piece
was inspired by the classic
architectural study Plug-in-City
(1964) by Archigram. User interactions create the virtual city in
physical and virtual civic space.
For example, when a user sits
on a park bench placed on the
site of the installation, a building
will appear in the projected city.
Plug-in-Play is based on the
concept that users, and the
community they inhabit, determine the success and structure
of cities. The installation, a clear
representation of communal
activity in space, premiered at
San Jose's City Hall in 2010.

LUNA MAURER

www.poly-luna.com

Amsterdam-based designer Luna Maurer crafts algorithmic systems, which she puts into motion and then observes as human input directs the outcome. Through careful constraints she triggers a sense of play in her participants. Maurer often collaborates with other members of the collective Conditional Design—Jonathan Puckey, Edo Paulus, and Roel Wouters. Her ensuing work flows between the tactile and the digital. She applies process thinking beyond the easy fit of programming, looking, as well, to physical actions—embroidery, applying stickers, hand-numbering—to create challenging frameworks for participation.

In what ways do you consider yourself a collaborative artist and designer?

I distinguish between two sorts of collaboration. One is collaborating by working together, as I do, for example, with my colleagues. We think of projects, make small workshops, and so forth.

This kind of collaboration through making, thinking of ideas or rules is a nice thing because we [at Conditional Design] have similar interests. We share some fascinations. Slowly we've formed the Conditional Design collective. We also work individually.

Using participants to produce a product, that is a different thing. That is gradually happening, because we like letting surprise into our work through input.

Do you mean embracing the unpredictable?

Yes, you can use the natural world for the input, but we increasingly use people. They are complex creatures, and you cannot predict how they will react. They talk back, react to your instructions or the tools that you give to them.

Is it a challenge to stimulate participants to contribute?

There are different gradations of how willingly users participate. We ask, does the task have the freedom and opportunity for users to put something from themselves into it? Or is it a rather computational task with limited possibilities for self-expression?

If there's too much freedom for the participants, then it becomes arbitrary and not engaging, whereas if there's too much limitation, there won't be enough possibility of expression. So it's a gradation—somewhere in the middle.

I don't mean, however, that the process automatically bores participants if there is little freedom. It doesn't have to be fun at the time for the participants to experience a thought-provoking project.

For example, in the *Oops…Fuck…* book project, participants numbered every page in the book by hand. [Fig 82] This repetitive task didn't involve much creativity. But people handled it in intriguing ways.

They developed little smart systems to pile up the paper, so they could do it more handily. They grew confused and made certain mistakes. We also considered the social effect the process had on the group while doing this together for a couple of days.

Documentation seems important to your projects, because they focus so much on the process. Can you speak to that?

Yes, documentation is part of the process itself. For example, sometimes we photograph every second of the making process. The final time lapse, the animation, reveals how the project evolves. We don't make it and then document it. I'm thinking here of the poster series on Conditional Design.

The members of Conditional Design get together every Tuesday night, set up rules, and then create something together. Would you classify that under collaboration or participation?

It's more like playing. Designing by playing games. And we are the players. But you could also set up the system and let other people play it. They would participate in the game.

In the Conditional Design meetings, have you ever come up with an exercise that just didn't work?

Well, none of them are perfect. There is an ideal of what we want, the perfect thing to make, which we haven't succeeded in yet. But failure doesn't exist, either. We find something provocative in each project.

For example, one could say, it's boring to draw one line for two hours, but, when we did this at a Conditional Design meeting, we had fun. [Fig 80] We considered the things we said to each other during the drawing, as well as the process itself.

The traditional goal of design is to communicate a message. But in your work, you put a system in play instead. Would you say that's true?

We build a framework, press the play button, and then gradually something processes, evolves, and then continuously changes as it goes on and on and on. I enjoy applying this idea to printed matter. Making systems that continuously process is easier with digital projects, of course. If you design a book, it's at the printer, and then it's done. So I have to apply my thinking in a different way to printed matter.

For example, I just designed a book in which the typography was stitched by a team of embroiderers. Following my instructions for connecting letterforms, they made all the text for the book. In that way I tried to apply these ideas.

Your work flows fluidly between tactile practices and digital practices. Can you speak to that?

My work flows through the physical and digital realm at the same time. My fascination lies here. All the thinking comes from my technological interest, but still, at the same time, I have a frustration about staying only within this digital context.

And what is that frustration?

In 2001 I did a project that was a grid. It was the website for the Sandberg Institute: www.sandberg.nl (still exists in the newer version). Once the user rolls over the grid, it gets distorted. I did that in Flash at the time, and I designed each distortion. And then, two years later, a friend said, "Hey, why don't we generate it?" A generative system, an algorithm... I loved it.

The first version was programmed, while the second had something edgy, a real-world relationship. Of course, it's a physical model, but it now involves something that doesn't feel programmed, something that is in between.

I want to combine the system and the logic with things outside the computer, illogical things. There is a tension there. I like to combine technology and the physicality of the dirty world.

Do you think in the future designers might become more creators of a process and less authors of a finished work of design? Do you think that's a necessary skill?

Today everything is in flux, people communicating back and forth with the design in real time. Therefore, designing tools for people to use is more logical than focusing on the end product.

When I teach my students, I want them to be aware of what is happening. But they should find out for themselves why they want to involve participation.

It should fit into the thing that they want to design, into the theme. Everything doesn't have to be collaborative. It depends on their own interests.

What reactions have you gotten from students when you teach them about process and parameters?

At one workshop, people had to execute things, and they didn't really understand what they were doing. But afterwards, when they had finished, or even a year later, they finally understood. Sometimes we really had to force them, you know: "Now we go into this limited freedom situation, and we do it together." At the Yale workshop specifically, I remember Roel and Jonathan telling the students, "You have to concentrate and execute it carefully; otherwise, it's not fun."

Even in our Conditional Design workshops, the careful, serious precision creates the tension that makes it compelling.

Your tendency to slow things down by increasing user concentration contrasts with the hyperspeed of our culture.

Yes. For example, in the Red Fungus project users (visitors of the museum) just have to place a sticker on the floor. [Fig 81] The moment they stick it, though, they have to think and react to what is already there. They must consider whether or not to do the same as the previous person, repeat a pattern, or behave in contrast to someone else. The more carefully users consider the options, the more they engage with it and grow excited about it.

This all has to do with real engagement. We're living in an overflow of participation, but it doesn't mean anything if you're not engaged with it. Yes, you interact when you click on a button, but you've forgotten about it the next second. Participation demands a little bit more.

Your projects craft a moment of real focus that participants must enter. It feels a bit meditative.

Yes, a good association. Absolutely. And it happens by itself. You don't need to go to a museum and stare at a painting. Here you discover things while doing them. That's really nice.

You write about building complexity from simplicity and relate this to a biological process. Could you talk about how your work relates to the natural cycles of the world?

This is, of course, the ultimate goal. From simple rules and ingredients, complex things can happen. Behaviors emerge—things that you haven't expected or predicted, maybe side effects that you didn't foresee. The system talks back to you. In fact, it designs itself.

That is the idea behind complexity theory. Complexity theory considers that simple modules have behaviors with certain characteristics. Once they interact, new characteristics emerge from them. This exists on all scales in our environment. You can design on a small-scale level, but once interaction happens, completely new complex phenomena will emerge.

What advice do you have for young designers today?

The outcome is not important. With our workshops, we try to do small experiments. Whether it's right or wrong, it doesn't matter. It's not possible to fail. Everything should be more like sketching, not this polished, finished thing. I could do my fungus project again, tweak it a little bit, but it's all one process of developing.

The other thing I try to teach my students is to look for what is interesting to them, rather than fulfilling an assignment or the needs of a client. Find out where your own fascinations lie and bring that into your working method. That is how you build ownership as a designer.

CONDITIONAL DESIGN

Fig 90 VITRUVIAN PAINT MACHINE, 2009
www.conditionaldesign.org

(right) Maurer and Paulus developed the Vitruvian Paint Machine for the 2009 Take on Me (take me on) exhibition in the Van Abbemuseum in Eindhoven, the Netherlands. The machine invited visitors to use Maurer and Paulus as a vehicle to create mural paintings, in accordance with specific rules. Visitors first picked a paint color, and then Maurer and Paulus contributed to the mural according to a preestablished algorithm.

Fig 91 4 LONG LINES, 2009
www.conditionaldesign.org

(left) This project represents one of the collective Conditional Design's weekly workshops. It was based on the following rules: Draw one line for one and a half hours without your pen leaving the paper. You may stop for a maximum of five seconds without lifting the pen. Don't cross another line.

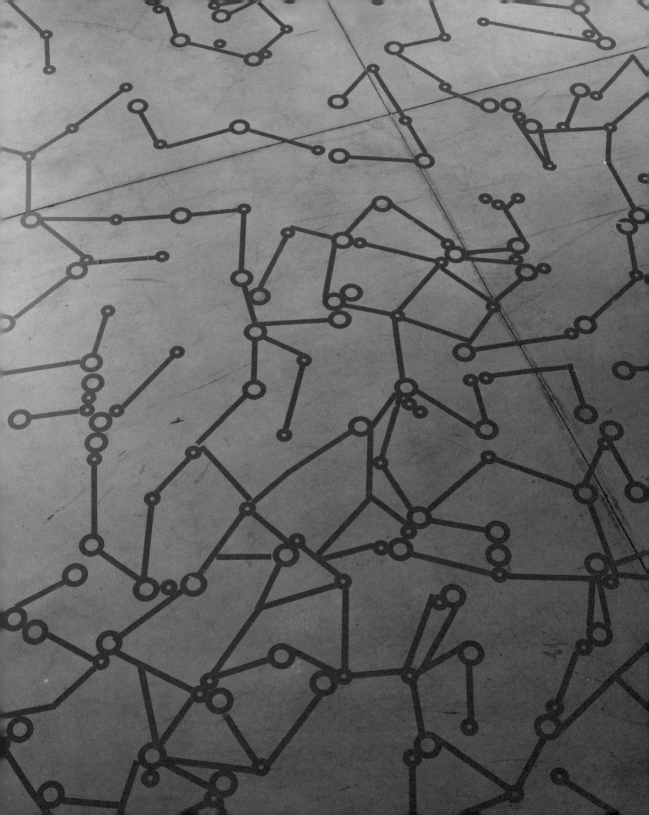

LUNA MAURER

Fig 92 **RED FUNGUS**, 2010
www.poly-luna.com

(opposite) Maurer created Red
Fungus as part of the 2010
exhibition Process as Paradigm at
LABoral center for arts and science
in Gijon, Spain. Upon entering the
museum, visitors received a sheet
of four stickers with the instruction
to affix them to the exhibition floor
according to a simple set of rules.
As noted by Maurer, "The show
reveals the elementary shift from
a culture based on the concept of
manifestation and the final product
to a culture of process resulting
from a networked society."[1]

1 Luna Maurer, "Red Fungus,
   2010," Luna Maurer website,
   http://www.poly-luna.com/red-
   fungus (accessed November 20,
   2010).

Fig 93 **HUH? OOPS...FUCK! OH...
OH, NO! WAIT...AGAIN...**, 2009
www.poly-luna.com

(right) Maurer developed this
graduation catalog for Media
Design and Communication at the
Piet Zwart Institute in collaboration
with Roel Wouters. Students, staffers, and designers hand-numbered
each of the book's forty-eight
thousand pages in two daylong
sessions. Each page number is
written in charcoal, allowing the
book to continue to transform as it
is being read. Through the continuing contamination of the charcoal,
Maurer transformed a physical artifact into an open-ended design.

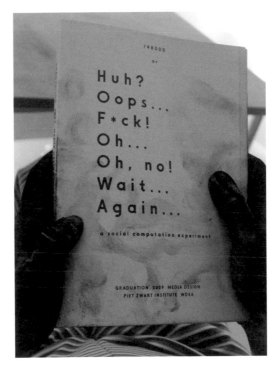

KARSTEN SCHMIDT

www.postspectacular.com

German-born Karsten Schmidt operates on the border between design and programming. He fits entirely in neither world, but excels in both. His work embraces the ethos of open source, offering knowledge gained through client work to the community at large. One outlet for this is Schmidt's growing code library, toxiclibs.org. (Online software design communities know him as Toxi). Schmidt's work, created through PostSpectacular, his studio, exemplifies the operative approach of generative design: "the shift from thinking about the (design) world filled with static objects and symbols to considering each one of them as the (intermediate) results of operations, processes, interactions causing them."

Can you identify a moment in which you shifted your focus from finished artifact to generative process?

A key moment was the beginning of my involvement in the development of Processing, the open source programming environment created by Ben Fry and Casey Reas, back in 2003. Back then, I was mainly using Macromedia Director and became increasingly frustrated with the corporate lack of long-term vision. I was searching for new tools and ways of working that I could help to develop myself.

When I started Post Spectacular in 2007, the idea was to develop a long-term project from scratch (toxiclibs.org), but use commercial and artistic project commissions as funding, both financially and thematically. Since then I've collaborated with people and companies in as many different fields of design as possible, in order to a) explore niches and find out what tools are lacking in these fields, b) learn myself about the design challenges there, and c) use concrete projects to develop solutions for these problems.

Since my work is heavily code-based, I can extract and generalize some of these solutions and add them to my collection of code libraries, which are then made available under an open source license to others. Over the past three years, the codebase of the toxiclibs project has grown to over 26,000 lines of code, making up over 280 different, interoperable building blocks for a variety of creative disciplines.

What's missing in design education right now?

Design education is too preoccupied with style, aesthetics, self-reference. It could be more focused on the understanding of interrelated systems and become more transdisciplinary.

Is graphic design moving toward obsolescence? Will generative processes replace designers?

The answer depends on how you define the discipline. In traditional design agency structures, some roles largely focused on design implementation/production will become obsolete through increased automation.

However, in a market-driven economy this happens to all fields, and we should not confuse automation with generative design. The concept of generative design is often misunderstood in the same way electronic music has been imagined by some people as just pressing a few buttons and the synthesizer magically produces an entire track. This couldn't be further from the truth.

Generative design involves more in the act of creation (or at least has the potential to) than other existing approaches. This is slightly paradoxical, since we seem to hand over much of the control to the machine. Here lies much of the source of this misunderstanding, namely the by now well-estab-lished cultural acceptance that the vast majority of the creative industry relies on tools produced by other parties "for them." Hence, any form of creating with computers is seen as handing over control to the machine. It's the mindset of a consumer society.

Discussions get sidetracked quickly by the preva-lent complex aesthetics in the generative design field, but they're just a symptom of the conceptual shift in the underlying approach: the shift from thinking about the (design) world filled with static objects and symbols to considering each one as the (intermediate) results of operations, processes, interactions causing them. At the heart, it's simply the acknowledgment of the time axis in every element, which in turn means to stop thinking about design elements as objects and start inquiring what processes could lead to certain outcomes. It's the traditional approach turned upside down, bottom-up.

To conceptually work with such a fluid, action-based philosophy, we need a medium to express and experiment with these highly abstract processes. The best medium we currently have in this respect is code, software. We need creative humans who can look beyond the stylistic novelties afforded by the genera-tive approach and are able to equally discover, model, encode, and mesh these processes and their rules of engagement into new solutions.

The benefit of working with actual processes (rather than their outcomes) is that they are paramet-ric and can be recombined, extended, and shaped in infinite ways. This recombination often produces excit-ing, unexpected results leading one on a meandering path of serendipity. Any person doing so will quickly find herself dissolving various artificial boundaries we have created in the field of design. Open source plays a key role in this respect, since it means the mental effort of encoding only needs to be done once (in principle) and then enables others to solve tasks

conceptually related, which might help ourselves in turn and so on. We might shed the designer label and become creators instead.

In your manifesto you state that the population is often more important than the individual. What do you mean by that?

There were several projects I've worked on for which the required outcome of designs was numbering in thousands of unique solutions. One of them was the design process of the book jacket system for the Faber Finds print-on-demand label. The motto of the design brief was to create infinite variation within a fairly con-strained art direction, initially provided as four border design templates by Marian Bantjes. [Fig 29] Infinite variation sounds great until one realizes that some variations are, of course, not as good as others, if even acceptable at all. We had to make any design decision in such a way that it simply reigned in the extremes, the weird cases. To make such decisions we have to work with the concept of multidimensional design spaces in which each parameter defines its own axis. By tweaking the range of each parameter individually, we can slowly shape the space of possible outcomes to suit our needs and ensure no unacceptable results are ever produced. Since most parameters are also interrelated, this is an often painstakingly slow (iterative) but worthwhile process.

The other example is the famous aphorism: "A rising tide lifts all boats." Frequently used by John F. Kennedy, but really an idea from game theory, the phrase is a statement about collaboration and sharing. There have been occasions where I person-ally "lost out" due to my willingness to share my knowledge with others, but I can't allow these events to affect my general support of open source culture, which I believe is conceptually the only sustainable way for us to move on (with notable exceptions, of course, where such a philosophy would be deadly).

KARSTEN SCHMIDT

Fig 83 **DECODE: DIGITAL DESIGN SENSATIONS IDENTITY**, 2010
www.postspectacular.com

(opposite) The V&A, in collaboration with onedotzero, commissioned Schmidt to create a generative festival identity for their landmark show Decode: Digital Design Sensations. The open source project included a public competition to remix and recode Schmidt's original identity. The winning recoded works appeared in an advertisement on CBS Outdoor's XTP screens, further promoting the exhibition. The identity application, its source code, a detailed user guide, and all other important information are available on www.code.google.com.

Fig 84 **LOVEBYTES GENERATIVE IDENTITY**, 2007
www.postspectacular.com

(right) In collaboration with the creative studio Universal Everything, Schmidt created a brand identity system and generator for the 2007 Lovebytes digital arts festival, with the theme "process," in Sheffield, United Kingdom. Schmidt began by isolating and defining a set of suitable design parameters and then chose value ranges for each, resulting in an identity system made up of around twenty thousand unique monster figures.

Fig 85 **ONEDOTZERO IDENTITY**, 2009
www.postspectacular.com

(left) This generative open source festival identity and large-scale interactive installation was designed by Schmidt for onedotzero, a London-based moving image and digital arts organization, and developed in collaboration with the advertising agency Wieden + Kennedy, London. The application was used to produce a trailer and posters for onedotzero's Adventures in Motion Festival, in addition to an interactive installation. The entire identity generator software, including documentation, is available as open source downloads on www.code.google.com.

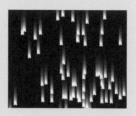

STUDENT WORK: *(from top left to bottom)* Jason Walters, Lauren Romano, Allison Backovski; Lauren Romano.

Print Design Systems, Miami University, fall 2010. FACULTY: *Jacob Tonski.*

Technology at Work

Building Complexity through Code

As design continues to embrace computation, designers are wresting control from corporate providers and making their own digital tools. One such pair of designers are Casey Reas and Ben Fry, who define their program, Processing, as "a structure for learning and exploration."[1] They designed it to teach the fundamentals of computer programming within a visual context, serve as a software sketchbook, and be used as a production tool.

    In this exercise, students at Miami University learned to manipulate typographic form through purely digital means using Processing. The results are fascinating images of computational spaces impossible to simulate by hand.

1 Casey Reas and Ben Fry, *Processing: A Programming Handbook for Visual Designers and Artists* (Cambridge, Mass.: MIT Press, 2007), 1.

TRY THIS PROJECT

Get set up. Download and install Processing from www.processing.org. Go to www.participatorydesign. net and download the Complexity Through Code file under Exercises. This will provide more specific instructions for the exercise outlined below.

Get started. Press the play button in the top left corner of the window. Type a few letters, and they will show up on the screen.

Make some changes. Remove some of the comment //'s on lines 50–53 and rerun the sketch. Start by enabling the fallDown() command, then spinAround(). Remove the // before line 36 or lines 38–39 and place a new // before the background command on line 34. This will make your letter fall down and spin around the screen. Repeat this step for each command to add interactive motion to your letters.

Make some more changes. Look at how each letter's initial position is established in the following lines. Line 61: void keyPressed() {
Processing executes the keyPressed section of the code each time you press a key. This action enables your program to respond to user input.
Line 65: curX = curX + 20;
In response to this line, Processing adds 20 pixels to the value stored under current X (curX). Change the number to 10. Note that the horizontal letterspacing grows tighter.

Empower your mouse. Change line 76 from: letters[letters.length-1] = new LetterForm(key, curX, curY, theFont); to: letters[letters.length-1] = new LetterForm(key, mouseX, mouseY, theFont);
By changing the terms *curX* and *curY* to *mouseX* and *mouseY*, you have changed the way a new letterform is created. Previously you were creating letterforms by pressing keys. Now you are adding functionality by using the mouse. As you type, move the mouse around on the canvas and watch your generative work in action.

TIMES 1000 7, 8, 9, 10, 11, 12, 13, 14, 15, 16, 17, 18, 19, 20, 21, 22, 23, 24, 25, 26, 27, 28, 29, 30, 31, 32, 33, 34, 35, 36, 37, 38, 39, 40, 41, 42, 43, 44, 45, 46, 47, 48, 49, 50, 51, 52, 53, 54, 55, 56, 57, 58, 59, 60, **Design a (semi) automated process to fill 1000 sheets of paper.** 81, 82, 83, 84, 85, 86, 87, 88, 89, 90, 91, 92, 93, 94, 95, 96, 97, 98, 99, 100, 101, 102, 103, 104, 105, 106, 107, 108, 109, 110, 111, 112, 113, **Think about the input, what happens to it during the process** 131, 132, 133, 134, 135, 136, **(the algorithm) and what the collection becomes as a result.** 153, 154, 155, 156, 157, 158, 159, 160, 161, 162, 163, 164, 165, 166, 167, 168, 169, 170, 171, 172, 173, 174, 175, 176, 177, 178, 179, 180, 181, 182, **You can work by hand, use a printer or design a custom invention.** 199, 200, 201, 202, 203, 204, 205, 206, 207, 208, 209, 210, 211, 212, 213, 214, 215, 216, 217, 218, 219, 220, 221, 222, 223, 224, 225, **How does a single sheet relate to all the others?** 238, 239, 240, 241, 242, 243, 244, 245, 246, 247, 248, 249, 250, 251, 252, 253, 254, 255, 256, 257, 258, 259, 260, 261, 262, 263, 264, 265, 266, 267, **Think of a good way to browse through this collection in the end.** 283, 284, 285, 286, 287, 288, 289, 290, 291, 292, 293, 294, 295, 296, 297, 298, 299, 300, 301, 302, 303, 304, 305, 306, 307, 308, 309, **- Fill 1000 pages of paper** 317, 318, 319, 320, 321, 322, 323, 324, 325, 326, 327, 328, 329, 330, 331, **- A4 or larger** 336, 337, 338, 339, 340, 341, 342, 343, 344, 345, 346, 347, 348, 349, 350, 351, 352, **- Automate the process** 359, 360, 361, 362, 363, 364, 365, 366, 367, 368, 369, 370, 371, 372, **- Each page should be unique** 381, 382, 383, 384, 385, 386, 387, 388, 389, 390, 391, 392, 393, 394, 395, 396, 397, 398, 399, 400, 401, 402, 403, 404, 405, 406, 407, 408, 409, 410, 411, 412, 413, **Algorithm: http://en.wikipedia.org/wiki/Algorithm** 426, 427, 428, 429, 430, 431, 432, 433, 434, 435, 436, 437, 438, 439, 440, 441, 442, 443, 444, 445, 446, 447, 448, 449, 450, 451, 452, 453, 454, 455, 456, 457, 458, 459, 460, 461, 462, 463, 464, 465, 466, 467, 468, 469, 470, 471, 472, 473, 474, 475, 476, 477, 478, 479, 480, 481, 482, 483, 484, 485, 486, 487, 488, 489, 490, 491, 492, 493, 494, 495, 496, 497, 498, 499, 500, 501, 502, 503, 504, 505, 506, 507, 508, 509, 510, 511, 512, 513, 514, 515, 516, 517, 518, 519, 520, 521, 522, 523, 524, 525, 526, 527, 528, 529, 530, 531, 532, 533, 534, 535, 536, 537, 538, 539, 540, 541, 542, 543, 544, 545, 546, 547, 548, 549, 550, 551, 552, 553, 554, 555, 556, 557, 558, 559, 560, 561, 562, 563, 564, 565, 566, 567, 568, 569, 570, 571, 572, 573, 574, 575, 576, 577, 578, 579, 580, 581, 582, 583, 584, 585, 586, 587, 588, 589, 590, 591, 592, 593, 594, 595, 596, 597, 598, 599, 600, 601, 602, 603, 604, 605, 606, 607, 608, 609, 610, 611, 612, 613, 614, 615, 616, 617, 618, 619, 620, 621, 622, 623, 624, 625, 626, 627, 628, 629, 630, 631, 632, 633, 634, 635, 636, 637, 638, 639, 640, 641, 642, 643, 644, 645, 646, 647, 648, 649, 650, 651, 652, 653, 654, 655, 656, 657, 658, 659, 660, 661, 662, 663, 664, 665, 666, 667, 668, 669, 670, 671, 672, 673, 674, 675, 676, 677, 678, 679, 680, 681, 682, 683, 684, 685, 686, 687, 688, 689, 690, 691, 692, 693, 694, 695, 696, 697, 698, 699, 700, 701, 702, 703, 704, 705, 706, 707, 708, 709, 710, 711, 712, 713, 714, 715, 716, 717, 718, 719, 720, 721, 722, 723, 724, 725, 726, 727, 728, 729, 730, 731, 732, 733, 734, 735, 736, 737, 738, 739, 740, 741, 742, 743, 744, 745, 746, 747, 748, 749, 750, 751, 752, 753, 754, 755, 756, 757, 758, 759, 760, 761, 762, 763, 764, 765, 766, 767, 768, 769, 770, 771, 772, 773, 774, 775, 776, 777, 778, 779, 780, 781, 782, 783, 784, 785, 786, 787, 788, 789, 790, 791, 792, 793, 794, 795, 796, 797, 798, 799, 800, 801, 802, 803, 804, 805, 806, 807, 808, 809, 810, 811, 812, 813, 814, 815, 816, 817, 818, 819, 820, 821, 822, 823, 824, 825, 826, 827, 828, 829, 830, 831, 832, 833, 834, 835, 836, 837, 838, 839, 840, 841, 842, 843, 844, 845, 846, 847, 848, 849, 850, 851, 852, 853, 854, 855, 856, 857, 858, 859, 860, 861, 862, 863, 864, 865, 866, 867, 868, 869, 870, 871, 872, 873, 874, 875, 876, 877, 878, 879, 880, 881, 882, 883, 884, 885, 886, 887, 888, 889, 890, 891, 892, 893, 894, 895, 896, 897, 898, 899, 900, 901, 902, 903, 904, 905, 906, 907, 908, 909, 910, 911, 912, 913, 914, 915, 916, 917, 918, 919, 920, 921, 922, 923, 924, 925, 926, 927, 928, 929, 930, 931, 932, 933, 934, 935, 936, 937, 938, 939, 940, 941, 942, 943, 944, 945, 946, 947, 948, 949, 950, 951, 952, 953, 954, 955, 956, 957, 958, 959, 960, 961, 962, 963, 964, 965, 966, 967, 968, 969, 970, 971, 972, 973, 974, 975, 976, 977, 978, 979, 980, 981, 982, 983, 984, 985, 986, 987, 988, 989, 990, 991, 992, 993, 994, 995, 996, 997, 998, 999, 1000

Times 1000

Experiment with automation. What does it mean to automate a process? When a machine performs previously manual labor, it is said to be automated. Graphics software has automated the fundamental tasks of the profession, such as setting type, composing layouts, drawing, and working with images.

In this assignment, designers and educators Luna Maurer and Jonathan Puckey explored automation and algorithm by asking students to design systems for efficiently creating content to fill one thousand pages.

(opposite) Luna Maurer and Jonathan Puckey, assignment sheet

STUDENT WORK: *(this page) Second year Graphic Design, Interaction Design Course, Gerrit Rietveld Academie, Amsterdam, 2010.* INSTRUCTOR: *Luna Maurer and Jonathan Puckey.*

start static **9**

Mass Customization

Customize and mass-produce at the same time. Publications are traditionally mass-produced, with each copy being exactly like the next. Added value comes into play only when an author signs or numbers a copy, thereby making it unique. Recently designers have begun to produce publications that are both mass-produced and custom one-off pieces. For example, Daniel Eatock's monograph *Daniel Eatock Imprint* (Princeton Architectural Press, 2008) includes an unvarnished area on the spine for his fingerprint. Eatock went to the warehouse storing his book and applied a fingerprint to each copy himself. Designer Luna Maurer created a publication in which the page numbers were written in by hand in charcoal. In both cases, the human touch contrasts with the anonymity of computer-generated design.

In this project, University of Miami students created literary publications, each with a different strategy of mass customization.

TRY THIS PROJECT

Select nineteen poems and create a literary journal containing the resulting compilation.

Use no more than two typefaces and two colors. All spreads should follow an assigned grid. Include a title and a concept for future issues of the journal.

Upload your design to Lulu to set it up for mass production.

Find a strategy to make each copy of the journal unique. Keep in mind that your concept must make each issue unique, but be efficient enough that it could conceivably be done with hundreds of publications.

Once you get your journal back from Lulu, customize it and share it with an audience.

STUDENT WORK: *(this page)*
Kristen Whaley, Erin Killinger,
Emily Drumm.
Print Design Systems, Miami
University, fall 2010. FACULTY:
Helen Armstrong.

STUDENT WORK: *(opposite)*
Haley Biel.
Print Design Systems, Miami
University, fall 2010. FACULTY:
Helen Armstrong.

The four projects featured here show different ways of customizing printed matter. In her journal, *Vicinity,* Kristen Whaley introduces a cover wrap, cut at a unique angle for each issue. The varied cuts reveal a different section of the cover in each iteration. The angles of the cover also inspire inside spreads. In another solution, Erin Killinger adds a hand-torn belly band to *Habitat,* her on-demand, digitally printed volume. A die-cut on the cover of *Sector,* by Emily Drumm, exposes a different, hand-stamped pattern on the first page of each issue. Finally, in Haley Biel's *Start Static,* a graphic pattern of static covers up portions of poems, completely obfuscating one specific poem in each iteration. In order to read the concealed text, the user must buy another issue.

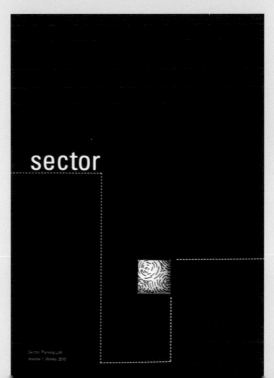

Technology Principles

Algorithm An algorithm is a mathematical set of instructions—a method—used to solve a problem. Most code is based on algorithms, but algorithms have existed long before computers. Designers use algorithms as the building blocks for creating generative designs.

Application or Program Smaller pieces of algorithmic code are the building blocks of larger, more complex operations called applications or programs. A program tells a computer what set of actions to perform in order to solve a problem. Programs have become commonplace, from word processing tools, to graphics applications, to mobile device applications, or apps.

"ALGORITHM = LOGIC + CONTROL."

ROBERT KOWALSKI, *COMMUNICATIONS OF THE ACM*, 1979

Fig 86 **EMERGENT TABLEWARE**, 2005
www.designercraftsman.com

In this project, designer Richard Elaver asks, "What if products are grown like trees, each a unique manifestation of underlying coded structure?" His Emergent Tableware consists of thirty-six individualized pieces. Elaver generated this silverware set using a computer program written to vary the form of each piece slightly. Finished pieces are cast from 3-D prints of CAD models.

WHAT IS MATH? [1]

A Four-Step Answer By Conrad Wolfram

1. POSE THE RIGHT QUESTION.
2. CONVERT YOUR REAL-WORLD PROBLEM INTO A MATH PROBLEM.
3   TURN IT INTO AN ANSWER IN MATHEMATICAL FORM (COMPUTER-ASSISTED).
4. BRING IT BACK TO THE REAL WORLD AND VERIFY.

1   Conrad Wolfram, "Teaching Kids Real Math with Computers" (lecture, "TEDGlobal 2010," Oxford, July 2010), http://www.ted.com/talks/conrad_wolfram_teaching_kids_real_math_with_computers.html.

Code/Decode

Stripped clean of the imperfection and metaphor of human language, code is a direct, unequivocal language, targeted toward the machine. Graphic design can reinvest code with humanity.

Algorithmic by nature, code contains rules for converting one piece of information into another representation of that information. In other words, a code is a set of instructions for performing an action, written for a machine, so that the machine can perform that action. By contrast, decoding is turning the outcome of a coded action back into the basic set of instructions used to enable its performance.

Code is secret language. Embedded deep within our civilization's roots, it has shaped both our communication and our law. The earliest codes date back to 50 BCE, when Augustus Caesar ciphered state secrets and dispatched them across the Roman Empire. Code became increasingly complex when in the fifteenth century Leon Battista Alberti argued that at minimum a second rule of encryption was needed to make code less prone to breaking.

Code, from Latin *codex*, meaning book, also refers to codes of conduct. Books of law can be seen as sources of social code. Today, however, *code* primarily means a set of instructions written for a machine. Ironically, the law is up in arms against digital code, struggling to define and interpret it.[2]

2 Friedrich Kittler, "Code," in
*Software Studies: A Lexicon,
Leonardo Books,* ed. Matthew
Fuller (Cambridge, Mass.:
MIT Press, 2008), 40–47.

Data The plural form of *datum, data* refers to pieces of statistical information that, when processed and analyzed, can lend meaningful insight into a particular problem. For example, census data is a raw collection of information about the population. When studied, organized, and compared, it can paint a meaningful picture of a society. Data processing is much easier when automated and performed by computers. Graphic designers are called to interpret data analysis in visually appealing and intelligible ways that audiences will easily understand.

Fig 87 **TOXICLIBS**, 2010
www.toxiclibs.org

Designers are looking to the
open source movement as a way
of negotiating code ownership.
Driven by a desire to share
his code, Karsten Schmidt is
building a library of scripts on
www.toxiclibs.org.

Generative design refers to work made using algorithms—sets of instructions for performing an action. Such work contains an element of randomness, as its form is configured by automated systems rather than a designer's intentional decision. The generative designer, working digitally or physically, focuses on setting up a system rather than fashioning each design solution discretely.

Fig 88 **DECODE: DIGITAL SENSATIONS IDENTITY**, 2010
www.postspecticular.com

Digital particles shift and coalesce on the screen into letters spelling the title of a 2009 exhibition at the V&A in London. Pushing the logo's elasticity further, members of the public were invited to remix designer Karsten Schmidt's work into forms of their own. The code can be accessed at www.code.google.com/p/decode.

Fig 89 **GRAPHIC DESIGN IN THE WHITE CUBE**, 2006
www.jonathanpuckey.com/projects/graphic-design-in-the-white-cube

Luna Maurer and Jonathan Puckey led a workshop of students through a set of rules to complete and customize by hand the half-finished posters for the 2006 exhibition Graphic Design in the White Cube in Brno, Czech Republic, disrupting the monotony of mass production with the welcome touch of the hand. This, too, is algorithmic work.

Internet versus the World Wide Web

As a network of web pages operating on the hypertext tag protocol (http), the World Wide Web operates within the Internet. The Internet is the overarching global context of connectivity running on the TCP/IP protocol. The Internet accommodates many other protocols in addition to http, such as those used by email servers, iPhone, and Skype.

Although it has since become decentralized, the Internet was developed in 1971 as an initiative of ARPA, a research branch of the Defense Department. Its precursor, the ARPANET, connected fifteen academic institutions across the United States. Today hundreds of millions of people depend on Internet connectivity for their social and professional communications.[3]

3   Bill Stewart, "Internet History—One Page Summary," Living Internet website, January 7, 2000, http://www.livinginternet.com/i/ii_summary.htm.

Fig 90 **TYPE & FORM**, 2008
www.postspectacular.com

Karsten Schmidt uses biomedi-
cal programming technologies
to "grow" letterforms with code.
For the cover of *Print Magazine*
(August 2008) he printed these
forms with a three-dimensional
printer, resulting in entirely new
sculptural form—tactile, but not
made by hands.

Typography: To and from the Screen

By the late twentieth century, typography had come
far from its origins in wood and metal, moving
through mechanical and photographic processes to
a bodiless life on the digital screen. Stripped of its
material underside, letterforms now glow at us from
our monitors, inviting amateurs and professionals
alike to effortlessly set them on the page. Recently,
however, there has been a return to the materiality of
type, evidenced in the work of designers who fluidly
move between digital and hands-on media.

Fig 91 **BEYOND**, 2010
www.fromkeetra.com

Keetra Dean Dixon used an
extrusion machine to make exag-
gerated letterforms out of clay.
This project, shown at the 2010
exhibition Re:Form School in New
York City, reasserts the delightful
physicality of type, using an old
machine in a new way.

Fig 92 **RIBBON FOLDER**, 2010
www.scriptographer.org

(top) This tool by Jonathan Puckey
allows for the easy drawing of
folded ribbons.

Fig 93 **DESIGN PROPOSAL FOR
NEW SWISS BANKNOTES**, 2005
www.scriptographer.org

(middle) Using Scriptographer,
Jürg Lehni, in collaboration with
Manuel Krebs (Norm), developed
this flexible image raster system
based on hexagonal grids. The
resulting design was entered
into the Swiss National Bank
design competition.

Fig 94 **AFTERNOW**, 2005
www.scriptographer.org

(bottom) In this project, Lehni
used Scriptographer to produce
a limited edition of posters
in collaboration with Philippe
Decrauzat. The resulting typography was inspired by 3-D type
on a 1973 record sleeve of *The
Faust Tapes*.

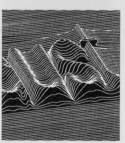

Technology Tools

Graphics software has been developing on two tracks. On the one hand,
programs are becoming consolidated under fewer and fewer manufacturers,
with competition dwindling due to corporate buyouts. On the other hand, there
has been a recent surge of small, directed applications focused on perfecting a
single task, created and offered by individual designers. These tools, downloadable from the Internet at no or minimal cost, are often driven by a designer's
passion for her or his craft, rather than by profit margins. Reliant on developers'
platforms such as Adobe Air and Processing, they stem from a collective desire
among designers to reclaim their tools and shape them to their own needs.
Following is a diverse sampling of currently available tools.

Scriptographer When Jürg Lehni launched Scriptographer in 2001, he introduced
it as a scripting plug-in for Adobe Illustrator that "gives the tool back into the hand
of the user and confronts a closed product with the open source philosophy."[4] This
plug-in, available for free (www.scriptographer.org), enables designers to create
tools that expand the formal capabilities of Illustrator. A more limited plug-in
prototype by digital innovator Drew Trujillo (aka Dr. Woohoo) allows for simultaneous co-creation with Illustrator (www.vimeo.com/11993533).

   As minimodules focused on performing one task well rather than overarching do-it-all programs, these tools foreshadow the future customization of
graphics software.

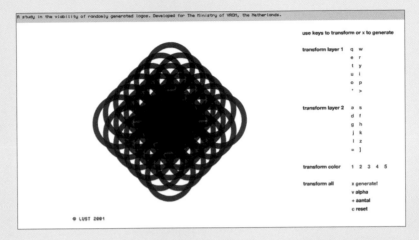

A study in the viability of randomly generated logos. Developed for The Ministry of VROM, the Netherlands.

use keys to transform or x to generate

transform layer 1	q	w
	e	r
	t	y
	u	i
	o	p
	*	>

transform layer 2	a	s
	d	f
	g	h
	j	k
	l	z
	=	]

transform color   1 2 3 4 5

transform all	x generate!
	v alpha
	+ aantal
	c reset

© LUST 2001

Fig 96 **MINISTRY OF VROM LOGO GENERATOR**, 2001
www.lust.nl

Fig 95 **MATHEMATICA**, 1988
www.wolfram.com/mathematica

While tools such as Scriptographer clearly add to a designer's skill set, others incite our latent fears of obsolescence in the face of digital advancement. The **Ministry of VROM Logo Generator** by the Dutch design firm LUST is an online tool for making logos using a balance of control and randomization. User-friendly keystrokes translate into mathematical parameters that guide the graphic form on the screen.[5]

Going a step further toward "self-design," **Mathematica**, a program for visualizing computation by brothers Steven and Conrad Wolfram, allows the user to enter simple parameters and watch a distributed array of graphic solutions appear on the screen.[6] Painstaking hours of drawing and comping have been obliterated in a second of computational power, begging the question: are such tools sending the individual designer to the dust bin of the past, or are they arming us with broader capabilities toward the client of the future?

4   Jürg Lehni, "About," Scriptographer website, http://scriptographer.org/about/ (accessed December 1, 2010).

5   LUST, "Ministry of VROM Logo Generator." LUST website, 2001, http://lust.nl/lustArchive/generator/index.html (accessed December 10, 2010).

6   Christopher Carlson, "Exploring the Tate Logo," Wolfram Demonstrations Project website, 2010, http://demonstrations.wolfram.com/ExploringTheTateLogo/ (accessed December 1, 2010).

BIBLIOGRAPHY

Aldersey-Williams, Hugh. *Cranbrook Design: The New Discourse.* New York: Rizzoli, 1990.

AIGA New York Chapter. *Fresh Dialogue 8: Designing Audiences.* New York: Princeton Architectural Press, 2008.

Anderson, Chris. *Free: The Future of a Radical Price.* New York: Hyperion, 2009.

Anderson, Chris. "In the Next Industrial Revolution, Atoms Are the New Bits." *Wired,* January 25, 2010. http://www.wired.com/magazine/2010/01/ff_newrevolution/.

Aranda, Benjamin, and Chris Lasch. *Tooling.* Pamphlet Architecture 27. With a foreword by Cecil Balmond and an afterword by Sanford Kwinter. New York: Princeton Architectural Press, 2005.

Baldwin, Carliss Y., and Kim B. Clark. *Design Rules, vol. 1, The Power of Modularity.* Cambridge, Mass.: MIT Press, 2000.

Barthes, Roland. *Image, Music, Text.* Translated by Stephen Heath. New York: Hill and Wang, 1977.

Benjamin, Walter. "The Author as Producer." In *Walter Benjamin: Selected Writings.* Vol. 2, part 2, *1931–34.* Edited by Michael W. Jennings, Howard Eiland, and Gary Smith. Cambridge, Mass.: Belknap Press of Harvard University Press, 2003.

Benkler, Yochai. *The Wealth of Networks: How Social Production Transforms Markets and Freedom.* New Haven, Conn.: Yale University Press, 2006.

Bierut, Michael, William Drenttel, and Steven Heller, ed. *Looking Closer 4: Critical Writings on Graphic Design.* New York: Allworth Press, 2002.

Bishop, Claire, ed. *Participation.* Documents of Contemporary Art. Cambridge, Mass.: MIT Press; London: Whitechapel, 2006.

Bourriaud, Nicolas. *Postproduction: Culture as Screenplay: How Art Reprograms the World.* Lukas & Sternberg series. Translated by Jeanine Herman. New York: Sternberg Press, 2002.

Bourriaud, Nicolas. *The Radicant.* Lukas & Sternberg series. Translated by James Gussen and Lili Porten. New York: Sternberg Press, 2009.

Bourriaud, Nicolas. *Relational Aesthetics.* Translated by Simon Pleasance and Fronza Woods with the participation of Mathieu Copeland. Dijon: Les Presses du Réel, 1998.

Bucher, Stefan G. *100 Days of Monsters.* Cincinnati, Ohio: HOW Books, 2008.

Burgess, Jean, and Joshua Green. *YouTube: Online Video and Participatory Culture.* Malden, Mass.: Polity, 2009.

Coles, Alex, ed. *Design and Art.* Documents of Contemporary Art. Cambridge, Mass.: MIT Press; London: Whitechapel, 2007.

Cova, Bernard, Robert V. Kozinets, and Avi Shankar. *Consumer Tribes.* Oxford, UK: Butterworth-Heinemann, 2007.

Cross, Nigel, ed. *Design Participation: Proceedings of the Design Research Society's Conference, Manchester, September 1971.* London: Academy Editions, 1972.

Davis, Stan. *Future Perfect.* 10th anniversary ed. Reading, Mass.: Addison-Wesley Publishing, 1996.

Drucker, Johanna, and Emily McVarish. *Graphic Design History: A Critical Guide.* Upper Saddle River, N.J.: Prentice Hall, 2009.

Eatock, Daniel. *Daniel Eatock Imprint.* New York: Princeton Architectural Press, 2008.

Fuller, Matthew, ed. *Software Studies: A Lexicon.* Leonardo Books. Cambridge, Mass.: MIT Press, 2008.

Galloway, Alexander R. *Gaming: Essays on Algorithmic Culture.* Electronic Mediations Series, vol. 18. Minneapolis, Minn.: University of Minnesota Press, 2006.

Gerstner, Karl. *Designing Programmes.* Teufen, Switzerland: Niggli, 1964.

Heller, Steven, and Véronique Vienne, eds. *Citizen Designer: Perspectives on Design Responsibility.* New York: Allworth Press, 2003.

Howe, Jeff. *Crowdsourcing: Why the Power of the Crowd Is Driving the Future of Business.* New York: Crown Business, 2008.

Jenkins, Henry. *Convergence Culture: Where Old and New Media Collide.* New York: New York University Press, 2006.

Jenkins, Henry, et al. *Confronting the Challenges of Participatory Culture: Media Education for the 21st Century.* Cambridge, Mass.: MIT Press, 2009.

Lasn, Kalle. *Culture Jam: The Uncooling of America.* New York: Eagle Brook, 1999.

Latour, Bruno. *Reassembling the Social: An Introduction to Actor-Network-Theory.* Oxford: Oxford University Press, 2005.

Lessig, Lawrence. *Free Culture: How Big Media Uses Technology and the Law to Lock Down Culture and Control Creativity.* New York: Penguin, 2004.

Lessig, Lawrence. *The Future of Ideas: The Fate of the Commons in a Connected World.* New York: Random House, 2001.

Lessig, Lawrence. *Remix: Making Art and Commerce Thrive in the Hybrid Economy.* New York: Penguin, 2008.

Levine, Faythe, and Cortney Heimerl. *Handmade Nation: The Rise of DIY, Art, Craft, and Design.* New York: Princeton Architectural Press, 2008.

Lévy, Pierre. *Collective Intelligence: Mankind's Emerging World in Cyberspace.* Translated by Robert Bononno. New York: Plenum Trade, 1997.

Lévy, Pierre. *Cyberculture.* Translated by Robert Bononno. Minneapolis, Minn.: University of Minnesota Press, 2001.

Lovink, Geert. *Zero Comments: Blogging and Critical Internet Culture.* New York: Routledge, 2007.

Lupton, Ellen, and Jennifer Cole Phillips. *Graphic Design: The New Basics.* New York: Princeton Architectural Press, 2008.

Lupton, Ellen. *Thinking with Type: A Critical Guide for Designers, Writers, Editors, & Students.* New York: Princeton Architectural Press, 2004.

Maffesoli, Michel. *The Time of the Tribes: The Decline of Individualism in Mass Society.* Translated by Don Smith. London: Sage, 1996. Originally published as *Le temps des tribus: le déclin de l'individualisme dans les sociétés de masse* (Paris: Méridiens Klincksieck, 1988).

Manovich, Lev. "Remixability and Modularity." Lev Manovich (blog), October–November 2005, http://manovich.net/articles/.

Marchand, Roland. *Creating the Corporate Soul: The Rise of Public Relations and Corporate Imagery in American Big Business.* Berkeley: University of California Press, 1998.

Maurer, Luna, and Roel Wouters. "Decoding and Graphic Design Seminar." Lecture, Graphic Design Festival Breda, Breda, the Netherlands, May 25, 2010.

Meadows, Donella H. *Thinking in Systems: A Primer.* Edited by Diana Wright. White River Junction, Vt.: Chelsea Green, 2008.

Müller-Brockmann, Josef. "Grid and Design Philosophy." In *Grid Systems in Graphic Design: A Visual Communication Manual for Graphic Designers, Typographers, and Three Dimensional Designers.* Niederteufen, Switzerland: Niggli; New York: Hastings House Publishers, 1981.

Opara, Eddie. "Insights Design Lecture Series: Eddie Opara." Lecture, Walker Art Center, Minneapolis, Minn., March 9, 2010. http://channel.walkerart.org/play/eddie-opara/.

Pine, B. Joseph. *Mass Customization: The New Frontier in Business Competition.* Boston: Harvard Business Press, 1993.

Pink, Daniel H. *Drive: The Surprising Truth about What Motivates Us.* New York: Riverhead, 2009.

Poynor, Rick. "First Things First Manifesto 2000." *AIGA Journal of Graphic Design* 17, no. 2 (1999): 6–7.

Prahalad, C. K., and Venkatram Ramaswamy. *The Future of Competition: Co-Creating Unique Value with Customers.* Boston: Harvard Business Press, 2004.

Puckey, Jonathan, "Trace a Face." Lecture, Konst & Teknik, Stockholm, Sweden, November 6, 2008.

Rancière, Jacques. *The Emancipated Spectator.* London: Verso, 2009.

Rattner, Donald. "Roundup: Mass Customized Food." *A.R.T. Blog,* July 8, 2010. http://www.art-rethought.com/blog/2010/07/roundup-mass-customized-food/.

Reas, Casey, and Ben Fry. *Processing: A Programming Handbook for Visual Designers and Artists.* Cambridge, Mass.: MIT Press, 2007.

Reas, Casey, Chandler McWilliams, and Jeroen Barendse. *Form+Code in Design, Art, and Architecture.* New York: Princeton Architectural Press, 2010.

Ritchie, Kevin. "Chris Milk Talks Crowdsourced Johnny Cash Project." *'boards,* April 28, 2010. http://www.boardsmag.com/community/blogs/behindthescenes/index.php?p=1236.

Rushkoff, Douglas. *Program or Be Programmed: Ten Commands for a Digital Age.* New York: OR Books, 2010.

Schmidt, Karsten. "Real Fake." Lecture, "Real Fake" symposium, University for Art and Industrial Design, Linz, Austria, May 28, 2010.

Simon, Nina. *The Participatory Museum.* Santa Cruz: Museum 2.0, 2010.

Stallman, Richard. "The GNU Manifesto." GNU Operating System website, last updated December 12, 2010, http://www.gnu.org/gnu/manifesto.html.

Sunstein, Cass R. *Infotopia: How Many Minds Produce Knowledge.* New York: Oxford University Press, 2006.

Surowiecki, James. *The Wisdom of Crowds: Why the Many Are Smarter than the Few and how Collective Wisdom Shapes Business, Economies, Societies, and Nations.* New York: Doubleday, 2004.

Tapscott, Don, and Anthony D. Williams. *Wikinomics: How Mass Collaboration Changes Everything.* New York: Portfolio, 2006.

Wolff Olins. "Brand Next." Wolff Olins website, March–July 2008, http://www.wolffolins.com/brandnext/.

Wolstenholme, Ben. "Weare Press Release." Weare website, November 2007. http://weare.movingbrands.com.

ACKNOWLEDGMENTS

Essential to this project are the many eminent designers who contributed their work. Thanks to all of them. I would also like to express deep gratitude to my colleagues at Miami University for their continuing support. In particular, Peg Faimon, Glenn Platt, Tom Effler, Samantha Perkins, and Jacob Tonski. Thanks as well to my students who provided a strong sounding board for this book in the classroom, never failing to inspire through their own energy and creativity.

To Ellen Lupton, a special thanks, for her generous spirit, insightful discourse, and unfailing encouragement. At Princeton Architectural Press, my gratitude goes to my editor Nicola Bednarek Brower for her thoughtful comments. And to my coauthor, Zvezdana Stojmirovic, for her incredible insight and co-creative spirit. Our collaboration inspired countless Skype conversations, emails, and meetings, all infused with the sticky fingers of small children. Finally, to my husband, Sean Krause, for his patience, love, and editing skills. And to my daughters, Vivian and Tess, who wake me each morning with laughter.

Helen Armstrong

My contribution to this book would not have been possible without the support of my students at MICA. Many of the practical examples on these pages are the result of their unbounded talent and curiosity. In addition, I am thankful to the leaders who make MICA the exceptional college that it is: Fred Lazarus, president; Ray Allen, provost; Jan Stinchcomb, dean for undergraduate studies and faculty; Ellen Lupton and Jennifer Cole Phillips, directors of the graphic design MFA program, and especially Brockett Horne, for her leadership of the undergraduate graphic design program. To Gunalan Nadarajan, vice provost for research, special thanks for supporting my course, Fashion Graphics, with a grant through the Office of Research.

Our editor, Nicola Bednarek Brower at Princeton Architectural Press, worked tirelessly to bring this book to fruition. Collaborating with my coauthor, Helen Armstrong, has been a joy and a privilege.

Finally, I'd like to lovingly remember my late parents, Milutin and Jelena Rogic. I thank my brothers, Predrag and Isihije, my husband, Aleksandar, and our sons, Milutin and the newborn Sava, for their encouragement and support.

Zvezdana Stojmirovic

CREDITS

Fig 2 courtesy Ellen Culpepper, photo by Sam Culpepper

Fig 3, 74, 93, 94 courtesy Jürg Lehni, Fig 3 *Things to Say*, Jürg Lehni & Alex Rich, Kunst Halle Sankt Gallen, 2009, furniture by Martino Gamper

Fig 4 courtesy Berber Soepboer and Michiel Schuurman, photo Sander Marsman, styling: Anne Stooker www.annestooker.com, model: Nina Varga

Fig 5, 23 courtesy Art House Co-op

Fig 6, 14 courtesy Daniel Eatock

Fig 7 courtesy Stefan Bucher

Fig 8 courtesy Troika

Fig 9 courtesy Moving Brands

Fig 10 courtesy SS + K

Fig 11, 15, 16, 17, 52, courtesy Project Projects

Fig 12, 32 courtesy MendeDesign

Fig 13 courtesy Winterhouse Institute

Fig 18, 28 courtesy Colle + McVoy

Fig 19 courtesy Sense Worldwide

Fig 20 courtesy Local Motors

Fig 21, 49, 61, 62 courtesy Post Typography

Fig 22, 54, 66, 68, courtesy Jonathan Harris

Fig 25 courtesy Graphic Thought Facility

Fig 26 courtesy Mia Cullin and Woodnotes Oy

Fig 27 courtesy Min Choi and Sulki Choi

Fig 29 courtesy Marian Bantjes

Fig 30 courtesy Brett Yasko

Fig 31, 86 courtesy Richard Elaver, Fig 31 photo by Swikar Patel, Fig 86 photo by Molly Reilly

Fig 33 courtesy Kvadrat, Ronan and Erwan Bouroullec

Fig 34 courtesy Linked by Air

Fig 35, 40, 41, 42, 92 courtesy Jonathan Puckey

Fig 36, 37, 38, 39 courtesy Aaron Koblin

Fig 43 courtesy LettError

Fig 44 courtesy Typotheque and Peter Bil'ak

Fig 45 courtesy Open Baskerville

Fig 46 courtesy Lars Müller, © Karl Gerstner

Fig 47 courtesy Eddie Opara

Fig 48, 58, 59, 60 courtesy Walker Art Center and Andrew Blauvelt

Fig 50 courtesy Mirko Ilić Corp.

Fig 51 courtesy Armin Vit and Bryony Gomez-Palacio

Fig 53 courtesy Catalogtree

Fig 55, 56, 57 courtesy Wolff Olins

Fig 63, 71, 75, 76, 77, 78, 91 courtesy Keetra Dean Dixon

Fig 64 courtesy Paula Scher

Fig 65, 72, 96 courtesy LUST

Fig 67 courtesy Nicholas Felton

Fig 69 courtesy J. K. Keller

Fig 70 courtesy Belle & Wissell, photos by Nikolai Cornell

Fig 73 courtesy Kram/Weisshaar, photo by David Levene

Fig 79, 80, 81, 82, 89 courtesy Luna Maurer, Fig 81 photo by Marcos Morilla

Fig 83, 84, 85, 88, 90 courtesy Karsten Schmidt

Fig 95 courtesy Steven and Conrad Wolfram

Thanks to all those who granted permission to reproduce their work. Special thanks to educators who shared images of student work: Clinton Carlson, Denise Gonzales Crisp, Nathan Davis, Brockett Horne, Jason Johnson, Jenny Kutnow, Ellen Lupton, Luna Maurer, Jonathan Puckey, Jacob Tonski.

Page 82 Ten Tips from *Crowdsourcing: Why the Power of the Crowd Is Driving the Future of Business* by Jeff Howe, © 2008, 2009 by Jeff Howe. Used by permission of Crown Business, a division of Random House, Inc.

INDEX